SCHOOLCRAFT COLLEGE LIBRARY
W9-BSU-707

The Art of Argument

The Art of Argument

GILES ST. AUBYN

Emerson Books Inc.
New York

Published 1962 by Emerson [illegible]

Library of Congress Catalog Card Number: 62-8865

First Printing, 1962

Second Printing, 1964

Manufactured in the United States of America

Contents

Acknowledgments

I am grateful to authors and publishers for permission to quote from the following books: *Clear Thinking*, R. W. Jepson (Longmans, Green & Co. Ltd.); *Thinking to Some Purpose*, L. S. Stebbing (Penguin Books Ltd.); *The Comforts of Unreason*, Rupert Crawshay-Williams (Routledge & Kegan Paul Ltd.); *The Psychology of Insanity*, Bernard Hart (Cambridge University Press); *The Proper Study of Mankind*, B. A. Howard (Ginn & Co. Ltd.); *Instincts of the Herd in Peace and War*, Wilfred Trotter (Ernest Benn Ltd.); *Principles of Social Reconstruction*, Bertrand Russell (Allen & Unwin Ltd.); and to the proprietors of *Punch* for some lines from *Save Your Seats*.

Introduction

Man's intellect has made him supreme among animals. Other creatures excel him in strength, size, and swiftness, but none in cunning. All his great achievements are the work of his mind, and knowledge has proved to be power. Many people naively assume that the mind is effortlessly logical, whereas, in fact, to be rational is not to comply with nature but to defy it. Thought, like all potent weapons, is exceedingly dangerous if mishandled. Clear thinking is therefore desirable not only in order to develop the full potentialities of the mind, but also to avoid disaster.

The first step toward straight thinking is to recognize the way in which the mind inclines to crooked thinking. A considerable part of this book is spent trying to show as simply as possible what it is that makes people irrational. To appreciate the dangers involved may not avert them, but it at least encourages caution. The main purpose of this work is not so much to provide the reader with lessons in logic as to persuade him that he requires them.

The need for clear thinking ought to be obvious. People who are confused or deluded cannot expect to understand the nature of situations in which they are required to act; and thus the decisions they make, being based on a false assessment of circumstances, are almost certain to be wrong. Opinions and actions that depend upon an appreciation of the world as it is and are reached by a process of rational argument are naturally more profitable than those derived from wishful or crooked thinking. It is a terrifying feature of democracy that vital issues should be decided by electors whose views are a compound of prejudice and ignorance.

To make students think logically has long been one of the aims of educators, many of whom have favored curiously oblique means of achieving this end. It is my belief that if one wishes to make students think logically one should teach them logic. The objection to this plan is that few simple books on clear thinking exist, and discussion about it has become very involved. Certainly the finer subtleties that interest philosophers are unimportant to those who have still to learn what is meant by "begging the question." This book attempts to fill the need for a brief, simple groundwork of logic. It contains no refinements and supplies only such information as everybody should possess. Whatever its faults, it is at least short. It is intended equally for the student and for any reader whose education in clear thinking has been neglected. The collector of taxes would be kept very busy depriving the author of his profits if everybody who came into this category bought the book!

I know that it is absurdly presumptuous to tell people how to be logical. Certainly nobody would benefit more from what follows than I would myself, if there were any chance of my being able to practice what I preach. My only qualification for discussing the subject at all is that introspection provides me with an inexhaustible fund of examples of crooked thinking. To keep the book short I have been dogmatic. The knowledgeable air I have assumed is not quite as ridiculous as it may seem, because, fortunately, the authority behind my pronouncements is seldom my own. I have leaned heavily for support upon: Hart's *The Psychology of Insanity,* Trotter's *Instincts of the Herd in Peace and War,* Jepson's *Clear Thinking,* Stebbing's *Thinking to Some Purpose,* and Thouless's *Straight and Crooked Thinking.* Anyone familiar with these works will recognize how much I owe them. They will appreciate, too, how sure are the foundations upon which this book rests. I am also much indebted to T. I. M. G. Beardsworth, E. W. Gladstone, and R. L. Ollard for the generous help they have given me. In conclusion, I must acknowledge the criticism of my students, who read the book in a rough draft and helped me to revise it.

GILES ST. AUBYN

I

Irrational Man

Perhaps the most astonishing of man's delusions is that he thinks he is rational by nature. In fact, reason, like virtue, is something of which he is occasionally capable but to which he does not often incline. The majority of men are governed by passion and prejudice, and their most confident judgments owe more to instinct than to argument. They have settled views on the origin, nature, and meaning of the universe. They know how the country ought to be governed and why it is going to pieces. They have strong opinions about heredity, the prevention of unemployment, and how to educate children. Since few who maintain these views can have the authority, knowledge, or experience to speak, it follows that many such opinions are based on inadequate evidence and are therefore to that extent unreasonable.

Psychologists regard the mind as an iceberg whose surface movements are determined by unseen forces below the water line. The visible part, consciousness, consists of those thoughts and feelings of which we are immediately aware: for example, the despair I feel as I struggle to explain a difficult concept in simple language, or the distaste for logic which the reader doubtless already entertains. Below the level of consciousness, but always ready to come to the surface, are a mass of memories, associations, and ideas. If I wish to recall the day of the week on which last Christmas fell, or my publisher's address, or the name of the man who murdered Lincoln, I may succeed in doing so by delving into the subconscious. Finally, far down in the depths of the mind is the territory of the unconscious. It shelters our primitive instincts, our automatic reflexes, our base emotions, and our suppressed memories.

The greatest achievement of nineteenth-century psychology was that it recognized the part the unconscious plays in determining our beliefs and behavior. The chief obstacle to studying the unconscious is that by definition it is something of which we are ordinarily unaware. If we examine our minds to see how they work, we are unlikely to notice the existence of unconscious processes; indeed, if we could they would not be unconscious. But it is sometimes possible to recognize in others what we cannot see in ourselves.

Lunatics provide exaggerated caricatures of ordinary people and their insane delusions have counterparts in everyday thinking. There is only a difference in degree between the patient who insists that he is a millionaire and the daydreamer who imagines he has inherited a fortune. The study of abnormal people, in whom ordinary processes have become enlarged and hence easier to observe, has enabled psychologists to understand the way in which normal minds work. It is from such investigations that we derive our knowledge of the unconscious.

The unconscious may be regarded as a region to which thoughts are banished or to which they escape. Because exiles are often trouble-makers, they are forbidden to return to consciousness; however, sometimes they contrive to evade the guard set over them. Realizing they will be extradited the moment they are recognized, they usually disguise themselves before slipping back over the frontier. Repressed memories and ideas often return from banishment during sleep. By stripping them of their disguises it becomes possible to discover their identity.

The following imaginary story shows how the process works. John Brownlow had a friend, Sebastian Butler, who became engaged to a girl whom John wished to marry himself. On hearing the news of the engagement, John was furious and momentarily contemplated killing his rival. Fortunately, discretion prevailed and he repressed the idea. That the thought should have crossed his mind need not surprise us. After all, two thousand years of civilization could scarcely abolish instincts acquired during a hundred millenniums of savagery. The night John heard that he had been supplanted by Sebastian he dreamt that he saw a person in livery struggling in a canal. After attempting to save the wretch from drowning, he discovered that the man was already dead. A crowd gathered and John heard people saying that he deserved a medal. His suppressed wish that his friend should die was satisfied in his dream. The man in livery was clearly a butler—Sebastian, in fact. Dreams often use puns as disguises. Whereas in waking life John was torn between the desire to have his rival out of the way and the remorse and shame of wishing him dead, the dilemma was resolved in the dream. Having attempted to save Sebastian, John had no need to reproach himself; on the contrary, as the crowd said, he deserved a medal. The banished wish returned disguised and found fulfillment in a dream.

Suppressed thoughts sometimes reveal themselves in slips of the tongue. A man once went to a party given by some rich friends of his and found that there was scarcely anything either to eat or drink. In the course of a political discussion with his host, he accidentally remarked of some statesman of the day, "He can at least be relied upon to give one a square meal." The assertion that "truth will out" shows considerable psychological perception.

The mind cannot endure conflict and is prepared to go to any length in the pursuit of harmony. Its policy is appeasement, and it is in the process of repelling thoughts and ideas that threaten to disturb its composure that it is most recklessly irrational or forgetful. Darwin, when he was working on *The Origin of Species* kept special notebooks in which he recorded objections to the principle he was formulating, because otherwise he found that he forgot them almost as soon as they occurred to him. Objections to his theory created mental disharmony and consequently his mind protected itself by tending to forget such disturbing ideas.

Another way of avoiding conflict is to rationalize, that is to say, to find or even invent reasons for behaving and believing as we do. Our moral conduct, for example, is largely determined by instinctive and unthinking obedience to religious traditions or class customs.

The ethical principles to which we appeal are often little more than afterthoughts designed to vindicate actions already taken. "It is a familiar fact that people of otherwise irreproachable honesty will swindle the government or a railway company with untroubled equanimity. If they are taxed with the incongruity between their principles and their conduct, a varied crop of rationalizations will be immediately produced. They will point out that a company is not the same thing as an individual, that nobody really loses anything, that the fares or taxes are so inequitable that it is justifiable to evade them, and so on." Whatever the number of reasons they find to justify their behavior, this much is certain: their conduct is not in fact determined by the principles to which they appeal.

The collision of opposing systems of ideas can often be avoided by keeping them apart. Thus an honorable man in private life can happily lie and cheat in business—provided he never allows the two spheres of actions to come together in his mind. This process of excluding incompatible ideas enables lovers to remain oblivious of each other's faults and explains the contrast between the precept and the practice of that part of mankind

> Whose life laughs through and spits at their creed
> Who maintain thee in word, and defy thee in deed.

Insane people are exceedingly adept at preventing contradictory systems of ideas from coming into collision. By keeping their delusions in separate logic-tight compartments they prevent them from ever confronting one another in the field of consciousness. The patient who believes she is queen of the universe contentedly scrubs the floor of her ward unperturbed by the incongruity involved.

Unfortunately, some contact between opposing systems of ideas can rarely be avoided. When this happens the mechanism of rationalization usually comes to the rescue and discord is averted. By means of rationalization the full significance of the situation is concealed and the relationship between opposing ideas is so distorted that their incompatibility is obscured. The man who has one set of rules for business and "another for private life probably persuades himself that to ask a customer three times the value of a certain article is obviously something quite different from thieving, that a man must live, and that the immorality of lying completely disappears when it is neccessary for the support of one's wife and family. Whenever, in fact, our actions conflict with our ethical principles, we seek for specious reasons which will enable us to regard the actions in question as a peculiar case altogether justified by the circumstances."

Abnormal people often resort to blatant rationalization. Patients suffering from delusions will, as far as possible, disregard facts incompatible with their beliefs, but if forced to face awkward facts, they will usually find specious arguments with which to conceal their significance. The lunatic who is convinced that people are seeking to kill him will distort the meaning of any event to make it fit his preconception. If he is treated kindly, then obviously a plot is afoot to lull his suspicions. If he is ill-treated, the hostility of his enemies is manifest. If he is given food, it contains poison; if he has nothing to eat, he is being starved to death. Similarly, the patient who maintains that he is a millionaire accounts for the fact that he has not a penny in the world by proclaiming that he is the victim of a conspiracy to deprive him of his money and estates. Forced to admit that he has neither rank nor fortune, the asylum tycoon persuades himself that envious relations have leagued together to deprive him of his inheritance. In the same way, many of the arguments which normal people adduce in support of their views are often masquerading as the cause of them. Indeed, much of our so-called reasoning consists in attempting to justify what we already believe. "We accept arguments as a drunken man leans on a lamppost, for support not illumination."

It is easiest to grasp general principles by considering particular instances of their working, and it may help to explain the process of rationalization if we refer once again to John Brownlow. John believes that literary critics earn a handsome living by preying on authors. Reviewers, so he maintains, herd together in contemptible little cliques, lavish praise on each other's trivial works, and ignore the promise of unknown writers whose originality they are unable to appreciate and whose talents they are quick to condemn. Moreover, critics are the parasites of the literary world, and the sooner they stop laying down the law and begin to realize that they are not omniscient, the better it will be for everyone.

It stands to reason that such people would not waste their time reviewing if they had the ability to write books themselves, and the fact that they make small fortunes from discouraging creative effort shows how dangerous they are. John is, of course, convinced that this attitude is forced upon him by the facts, but possibly the rough handling his first novel received from the reviewers has something to do with his dislike of them. Their censures very naturally galled him. His pride was hurt, and the disagreeable things they said threatened to conflict with his self-esteem. Unconsciously his mind began to seek ways in which to restore harmony. Soon, he discovered reasons for ignoring hostile criticism and persuaded himself that his book was a work of unrecognized genius destroyed by the envious malice of bigoted critics. Many of his objections to reviewers are not without substance. There is evidence for thinking that fine writing is occasionally overlooked, and equally there are good reasons for supposing that some critics have failed as authors. But the point is that the reasons John gives for distrusting reviewers, whether valid or not, do not explain his attitude to them. He does not dislike critics for these reasons. On the contrary, he produces these reasons because he dislikes critics. If John were fully conscious of the mental processes described above he would be guilty of hypocrisy; but as he is unaware of the true source of his opinions, and, moreover, fondly believes them to have been reached by carefully reasoned argument, we can acquit him of the intention to deceive. The comforts of self-delusion, however, tend to be short-lived, for stubborn reality has a savage way of destroying a fools' paradise. This side of the lunatic asylum one cannot go on believing only what one wants to believe. Truth will out.

The phenomena of post-hypnotic suggestion provide an excellent illustration of the way in which people manufacture explanations in order to disguise their real motives for behaving or believing as they do. In some way, as yet not fully understood, it is possible under hypnosis to establish direct contact with the unconscious mind. If a hypnotized person is told to turn a chair upside down after awaking from his trance and, moreover, is ordered to forget the source of this instruction, not only does he do exactly as bidden, but if challenged to explain his behavior finds an apparently good reason for it: for instance, that he wanted to see if the maker's name was stamped underneath. Not recognizing the origin or nature of the impulse by which he was moved, he invents an explanation with no conscious intention of deceiving himself or others.

Orders and ideas carried from hypnosis to waking life are called "continuative suggestions," and it is very instructive to see how people who have been subjected to them account for their subsequent behavior. A hypnotized subject was once told that when he awoke he was to take a flowerpot from a window sill, wrap it in a cloth, put it on a sofa and bow to it three times. After he had faithfully carried out these instructions he was asked his reason for performing so curious a ritual. The weather, he replied, was cold and it occurred to him that unless the flowerpot was warmed, the bulb might die. So he wrapped it in the cloth and put it on the sofa to be near the fire. As that idea delighted him, he bowed to acknowledge it. His real motive for behaving as he did was an unconscious urge, in this instance planted in his mind by the hypnotist, but being unwilling to admit that he had acted on mere impulse, he rationalized his conduct. It is difficult to resist the conclusion that a great part of our reasoning is of this kind.

One of the commonest causes of mental conflict is frustration of our instincts and desires. We want a holiday but cannot afford one. We would like to cheat but know that it is immoral. As usual, the mind has ways of dealing with such problems. One method it employs is fantasy. A small boy is unlikely to fulfill his ambition to drive an engine, so he pretends to drive one. In the same way, dreaming vicariously satisfies desires which everyday life is unlikely to indulge. Plays, novels, and films help us to fulfill in imagination what we cannot enjoy in reality. Occasionally, people try to solve their problems by utterly surrendering to fantasy. Rather than admit their own inadequacy, they protect their self-esteem by imagining they are of great importance.

Asylums are filled with emperors and millionaires who have paid this terrible price for equanimity. "Fantasy thinking" enables us to believe improbable stories on insufficient evidence simply because we want them to be true. "The trouble with most folks is not so much their ignorance, as their 'knowing' so many things which ain't so." During the first World War, when reinforcements were desperately needed, millions of Englishmen were comforted by stories about Czarist troops having landed in Scotland. Russian rubles, it was alleged, were found in slot-machines and foreign-looking soldiers turned up in several parts of the country with snow still on their boots. Any rumor, however improbable, was believed, provided it was heartening. But, as Bishop Butler once said: "Things and actions are what they are, and the consequences of them will be what they will be; why then should we desire to be deceived?"

Herd instinct is perhaps the most formidable of the unconscious impulses that influence our thought and behavior. Nearly everybody finds it intolerable to entertain ideas that differ radically from those generally accepted. The few who dare to maintain novel principles have not only to resist the persecution that nonconformity usually provokes, but also to fight against their own innate herd instinct. The printed word is credulously accepted because it bears the seal of herd approval.

The desire to conform is unreasonable because it encourages us to accept opinions without evidence and to assume that views prevalent in the community in which we live are so obviously true as to demand no further thought. Thus, English ladies who wear rings in their ears regard it as barbaric of African ladies to wear rings in their noses. Anything which tends to emphasize difference from the herd, or from a herd within the herd, is nearly always disagreeable. People are only too inclined to regard novel thoughts and actions as "wicked," "undesirable," or "bad form." "When we find ourselves entertaining an opinion about the basis of which there is a quality of feeling which tells us that to inquire into it would be absurd, obviously unnecessary, unprofitable, undesirable, or wicked, we may know that the opinion is a nonrational one, and probably, therefore, founded upon inadequate evidence."

Herd instinct is deeply ingrained in the very structure of our being, and a thousand years of comparatively civilized existence has done nothing to reduce its power. It is part of our animal inheritance. How advantageous social habits are in the struggle for survival is shown by the fact that a pack of wolves can kill a tiger. It acts as one but with the strength of many. To work together successfully, however, individuals must be sensitive to the behavior of their fellows; in other words they must possess herd instinct.

Gregarious animals, even when living alone, persist in behaving as if they were part of a herd. In domestication dogs retain the attitude toward food which their ancestors acquired when they hunted in packs. They eat hurriedly and growl anxiously if approached and they still "wolf" their food, although there is no longer any necessity to snatch what they can of the common kill. Man in this respect is little wiser than the dog. He too shows signs of gregariousness even when alone, and he is just as slow to discard traditional ways of doing things. It is alleged, for example, that solitary English travelers change for dinner in the jungle. The way in which early motor cars resembled the carriages they superseded also shows the persistence of ancient and outmoded habits. For that matter, almost any British institution serves to illustrate this point.

Man's gregariousness makes him fearful of physical or mental solitude; it makes him remarkably susceptible to leadership; and it subjects him to mob passion and panic. Its effect on his thinking is nearly always damaging, for it encourages him to accept without reason or evidence whatever the herd dictates. This would be less disastrous if majorities were more often right.

Most great advances in history have been made by men of genius, eccentric figures who refused to accept what their contemporaries regarded as obvious and self-evident. It is because these rare individuals have frightened the herd by their strangeness that many of the world's greatest benefactors have been persecuted or put to death. Originality has often proved a fatal infirmity. "Truth," said Milton, "never comes into the world but like a bastard, to the ignominy of him that brought her birth."

Man is so far from being reasonable by nature that if he ever achieves rationality, he does so because he contrives to offset the influence of unconscious impulses, because he manages to refuse the temptation to accept harmony at any price, and because he succeeds in resisting the desire to conform. In short, to be reasonable is not to comply with nature but to defy it.

2

Prejudice

A prejudiced person is one whose opinions are preconceived; he forms them without paying due attention to the evidence. The only reasonable ground for holding a belief is that the facts require us to do so. To be guilty of prejudice is to have jumped to unwarrantable conclusions, to believe what it is comfortable to believe, or to let thinking be influenced by feeling.

My opinion that writers deserve tax relief on the profits earned from their books is obviously suspect, since in considering the problem I am likely to have allowed irrelevant personal considerations more weight than they deserve. The fisherman who persuades himself that a salmon feels nothing after having swallowed a hook may be right but is nevertheless prejudiced, since he believes as he does not because the facts dictate the conclusion, but because the possibility that he derives pleasure from a cruel pursuit is too disagreeable to be contemplated. The following statement, made by a distinguished horseman, raises the suspicion of prejudice: "Hunting is really kindness to the fox. Instead of being the scum of the earth —as low in the opinion of man as the rat—he has become almost a king, respected by nearly everyone." The reason that juries are never allowed to know about the previous convictions of accused persons is that it would be almost impossible for them, if they were so informed, not to prejudge the issue. Knowledge of a prisoner's past would inevitably color his trial, and innocent people would be found guilty on the principle of hanging the dog with the bad name.

The achievements of scientific method show what can be done by disciplined thought. Scientists owe much of their success to their ability to face facts fearlessly and disinterestedly. They recognize the danger of rejecting evidence because it proves inconvenient, or accepting it because it conforms to their preconceived opinions. Darwin, for instance, refused to allow the Biblical account of the creation to affect his inquiry into the origin of species. Had he started his investigation assuming that every word of the Book of Genesis was literally true, he might easily have been tempted to ignore a mass of awkward evidence and select only those facts that confirmed his beliefs. In other words, he would have prejudged the issue. But, fortunately, he refused to impose upon nature preconceived theories and was not prepared to believe anything that his research did not compel him to accept. Consequently, instead of finding new reasons for maintaining old fallacies, he made a series of wonderful discoveries. Many of his opponents, however, were incapable of such impartiality. Darwinism appeared to them a flagrant and impious defiance of God's revealed truth, and they rushed to the defense of the traditional view of creation, heedless of the evidence which Darwin had collected. Their headstrong behavior displayed all the signs of partiality: a refusal to face facts, an anxiety to maintain comfortable doctrines, and a reluctance to modify traditional opinions. Moreover, the very passion that inspired their opposition showed how seriously their prejudices had been threatened. Their furious invective stands in marked contrast to Darwin's cautious and dispassionate logic.

The roots of prejudice often lie buried deep in the unconscious and to dislodge them is profoundly disturbing—hence the vehemence with which they are protected and the rationalizations they inspire. "Earthy minds, like mud walls," wrote John Locke, "resist the strongest batteries; and though, perhaps, sometimes the force of a clear argument may make some impression, yet they nevertheless stand firm, and keep out the enemy, truth, that would captivate or disturb them."

What Darwin said was uncomplimentary, for he insisted that man was just an animal closely related to the ape. This proposition alone suffices to account for the ferocious resistance he provoked. But worse was to come, for he dared to maintain that the world was older than the Bible implies, and that animals, far from being created in a single day, had taken millions of years to evolve. This terrible heresy was regarded by many people as a direct assault on the sacred opinions of the church, whose authority, it was alleged, would be undermined if such views ever prevailed. So from countless pulpits dazed congregations were warned that an infidel biologist (Darwin was, in point of fact, a Christian, but it was no time to be overscrupulous about details) had published a blasphemous book which aimed at the subversion of the church, the destruction of theology, and the rejection of morality. Many excited and agitated people never even momentarily considered the evidence for evolution, so horrified were they at the very thought of believing anything unorthodox. After a long and tempestuous struggle, Darwinism was accepted and the church readjusted its teaching to embrace the new doctrine. When the embers of controversy had at last turned to ash, people began to realize that God could hardly be offended by intellectual honesty, and that to seek truth wherever it led was to comply with His will.

The theological battle waged against evolution displays men's fear of thought. "Men fear thought," according to Bertrand Russell, "as they fear nothing else on earth—more than ruin, more even than death. Thought is subversive and revolutionary, destructive and terrible; thought is merciless to privilege, established institutions, and comfortable habits; thought is anarchic and lawless, indifferent to authority, careless of the well-tried wisdom of the ages. Thought looks into the pit of hell and is not afraid. It sees man, a feeble speck, surrounded by unfathomable depths of silence; yet it bears itself proudly, as unmoved as if it were lord of the universe."

Man's love of "a quiet life" and his resistance to anything that threatens his mental harmony account for his dislike of change. He is a creature of habit whose ways of thinking are thrust upon him. He is taught from infancy to accept the prevailing ideas of his age, the traditions of his class, the customs of his country, and the opinions of his family. In later life, he looks back on the world in which he grew up as the best of all possible worlds, and describes his youth with discriminating forgetfulness as the "good old days." So accustomed does he become to his own modes of thought and behavior that it never occurs to him that there is anything arbitrary in the habits he has acquired. Englishmen abroad, for example, have been heard to complain that the traffic travels on the wrong side of the road, that menus ought to be written intelligibly (i.e. in English), that it is disgusting to eat snails, and that foreigners have no sense of humor. Such people assume, without thinking, that there is no other view than that which they happen to enjoy. Since from their particular standpoint only one facet of truth is revealed, they fail to realize how different it looks if observed from another angle.

Institutions that have existed unchallenged for years or even centuries acquire an artificial sanctity that makes it sacrilege to criticize them. When William Willett proposed that the clock should be put back to save daylight, he was treated with universal derision. Every sort of objection was put forward to prove that his idea was blasphemous, lunatic, or impractical; the real objection, of course, was that his proposal required a revision of accepted ideas. How blinded by prejudice it is possible to become is shown by the fact that resistance was even offered to the introduction of anesthetics. Galileo, Copernicus, Newton, Darwin, Freud, and Einstein all challenged settled opinion, all met with bitter opposition, and all ultimately won acceptance. Despite our knowledge that most of the great advances in history have been made by rejecting "obvious" truths, we nevertheless cling uncritically to traditional beliefs. It was once "obvious" that the heart was the organ of thought. It was "obvious" that the world was the center of the universe. It was "obvious" that some men were slaves by nature and it was "obvious" that kings were chosen by God. For hundreds of years these beliefs were taken for granted, not because there was evidence to support them but because they were regarded as settled questions.

People are unable to bear the suspense of judgment that reason often demands, for they find it intolerable to live in a world that does not make sense. They are frightened of the unfamiliar and the unintelligible and they crave for what is known, certain, and safe. Because the mind nearly always finds the comfort it seeks, questions that should remain open become settled, and the skepticism that the evidence demands is discarded as unsatisfying. "In fact, one may say, paradoxically, that it is the desire to be rational which leads us as often as not to be irrational. We feel safer in proportion as we are certain that we understand the things with which we have to deal. One has only to think of such-and-such a political or moral or aesthetic controversy, and of the number of disputants who believe with passionate conviction that they understand the problem involved, to realize that most of them must be sadly mistaken in their belief. There are, of course, a number of possible motives behind their passionate conviction, but one of them is the desire to avoid the discomforts and uncertainties of the fundamentally skeptical attitude which remains constantly aware of the fact that opinions on such subjects can seldom be more than opinions and that few things are as simple as we would like them to be."

The instinct of self-preservation is one which man shares with every living creature and it is not surprising that so basic an urge should exert a profound influence on his thinking. Our desire to preserve ourselves extends far beyond the simple wish to survive. The same instinct that encourages a tigress at bay to fight until she drops may be seen in a modified form in many hotels and boarding-houses, where ladies of good family who have fallen on hard times battle to preserve the relics of their gentility as if to do so were a matter of life and death. It is almost impossible to prevent our love of power, wealth, and possessions from interfering with our judgment. There is a story that shows how difficult it is to remain detached when our personal interests are threatened. A Yorkshire man once tried to explain to a friend what Communists believed, and did so by telling him: "If tha had two houses, tha gives one to those that has none." His friend happily assented. "And if tha has two cows, tha gives one to thy neighbor that has none." Again the proposition won ready acceptance. "And if tha has two pigs . . ." "Nay, lad," protested the other, "tha knows I have two pigs."

The laws of most countries recognize that self-interest makes men susceptible to prejudice. In England nobody may vote at a council meeting who has a financial interest in any contract under consideration, and a member of Parliament who supported a motion financially beneficial to a firm of which he was a director would risk heavy penalties. Magistrates have to retire from the bench if a case comes before them in which their friends, business associates, or relations are involved, and countless precautions are taken in civil and criminal trials to eradicate prejudice wherever possible.

Saint Paul's attack on the goddess Diana, whom the Ephesians worshiped, shows what happens when vested interests are threatened and settled questions reopened. Demetrius, a silversmith by trade, whose living largely depended upon manufacturing idols, was disturbed by Saint Paul's condemnation of Diana, and so decided to address a meeting of his fellow craftsmen. He began his speech with a blatant appeal to their pockets. "Sirs, ye know that by this craft we have our wealth." He then played on their professional pride. "Moreover ye see and hear, that not alone at Ephesus, but almost throughout all Asia, this Paul has persuaded and turned away much people, saying that they be no gods which are made with hands, so that not only this our craft is in danger to be set at nought, but also that the temple of the great goddess Diana should be despised and her magnificence should be destroyed, whom all Asia and the world worshipeth."

This last statement was a wild exaggeration, but Demetrius was more concerned with the effect of his remarks than with their accuracy, and his audience reacted as intended. "When they heard these sayings they were full of wrath and cried out, 'Great is Diana of the Ephesians.'" Their anger, of course, was a sign that their interests had been seriously undermined. When Alexander, one of Saint Paul's supporters, tried to answer Demetrius, he was prevented from speaking by the crowd who "with one voice about the space of two hours cried out 'Great is Diana of the Ephesians.'" They were not prepared even to hear the arguments on the other side, but preferred to shout their slogan over and over again, thereby silencing their opponent. Moreover, many people probably began to believe what they heard so often. The episode illustrates what happens when cherished beliefs are challenged. We get irritated and pugnacious, we find arguments, not always valid ones, to vindicate our beliefs, and we encourage ourselves by chanting slogans. It might almost be argued that the more strongly we feel about an opinion the less likely we are to believe it for the reasons we give.

Nearly all our instincts can contribute to creating

or maintaining bias. It is no accident that pride, for example, leads to prejudice. We are often loth to accept the possibility that we are wrong, for no better reason than that to do so exposes our intellectual inadequacy. We are only too ready to combat criticisms of our views, however telling such objections may be, simply because to admit error is an admission of fallibility. "If we are told that we are wrong we resent the imputation and harden our hearts. We are incredibly heedless in the formation of our beliefs, but find ourselves filled with a passion for them when anyone proposes to rob us of their companionship. It is obviously not the ideas themselves that are dear to us, but our self esteem which is threatened."

There is a close connection between the prejudices of ordinary people and the delusions of the insane. Both are supported by rationalizations and both are impervious to argument, mainly because arguments are not directed against the real causes of the beliefs. If we attempt to reason with a lunatic we may easily provoke an outburst of furious rage or violence, a reaction not unlike that which ordinary people display when beliefs necessary to their mental comfort are challenged. Nearly all emotions tend to warp our judgment and the presence of strong feelings is a sure sign that irrationalism is near at hand. Being shocked, like being angry, is often a device to avoid facing facts. Hatred, fear, pride, and love make dispassionate reasoning difficult or impossible.

Love, as is well known, is very shortsighted and the prejudice inspired by patriotism reveals just how blind it can become. People often talk of their country in a deplorably arrogant way. They assume that it can do no wrong and that in any dispute it is always the other side that has erred. Patriots in wartime behave more crazily than many certified lunatics. During the first World War it was thought to be tacit treason to admire the works of Beethoven. Between 1939 and 1945 the British Broadcasting Company restricted broadcasts of Wagner's operas because Hitler liked them and because some of the composer's political ideas anticipated Nazi doctrine.

In an international dispute in which Britain is involved most Englishmen assume that their country must be right and that to consider the evidence would be to waste time. The passions which such disputes provoke are of the same kind as those which victims of delusions display when their invincible prejudices are menaced. An impartial survey of British history, even in the nineteenth century, shows many wrongs committed by Englishmen: the exploitation of backward races in which they excelled, the infamous opium wars, the callous indifference to human misery that successive governments displayed, and a mass of other evils of which they should be ashamed. When Professor Laski suggested that Britain was no longer a first-class power, a storm of protest arose. Yet what he said was the truth, disagreeable as it was to hear. Clearly, it is far pleasanter for the country to believe that it is the greatest power on earth, as it undoubtedly was a hundred years ago, than it is to face the fact that other nations have surpassed it in power and wealth. Laski presented people with an unpalatable truth and consequently they were shocked, indignant, and angry.

The ability to reason declines as emotion increases. If we are frightened, or in love, we can hardly expect to remain detached, and the more inflamed we become, the less able we are to think clearly. According to Shakespeare, the Earl of Westmorland remarked very sensibly before the battle of Agincourt:

> O! that we now had here
> But one ten thousand of those men in England
> That do no work today.

Considering that the English army was dangerously small, reinforcements would have been of the greatest value. Yet Henry V rebuked the Earl and told him that it was far better to fight a battle with a small army than a large one because as the outcome was already decided by God, it mattered not what size the army was.

> If we are mark'd to die, we are enow
> To do our country loss; and if to live,
> The fewer men, the greater share of honour.
> God's will! I pray thee, wish not one man more.

The King's speech, no doubt, was excellently suited to the occasion, because all he intended to do was to put courage into his troops, but had he allowed such considerations to influence his strategy, he would have been a lamentable general and a very deficient thinker. If great thoughts rise from the heart, it is better, as Lord Morley once observed, that they should emerge from the head.

It is much easier to detect prejudice in other people than it is to recognize it in ourselves. Indeed, prejudice would cease to exist if we could only recognize that the allegedly rational arguments upon which we claim to rest our opinions are as often as not mere afterthoughts that in no way explain the real motives determining our beliefs. The man who suffers from a fatal disease but refuses to believe that he is going to die, because the fact is too unpleasant to face, is obviously incapable of impartiality when it comes to assessing his symptoms. Having prejudged the issue he will naturally tend to force the facts to confirm his theory. We are unlikely to realize that we deceive ourselves when our wish for wealth and comfort or our dread of ruin and death leads us to believe propositions which, if true, would secure the objects we desire or avert the disasters we fear.

It is easy to see that others tend to believe what they desire or need to be true, and to disbelieve what they desire or need to be false, but to recognize the same processes at work in ourselves would be to discard prejudice, and a human being without prejudice is as common as a leopard without spots. It is simple enough for the Conservative to see that communism is an expression of envy and that its philosophy is one of greed, but it is another matter for him to realize that his own political faith may spring from self-interest and that his creed reflects his desire to retain the largest share of the cake. Of course, our motives for holding a belief do not affect its truth or falsehood. One can be prejudiced and right, but to be right for the wrong reason is a fortuitous way of arriving at truth.

Prejudice may provoke any of the thousands of logical errors of which man is capable, but, in particular, it encourages rationalization and partial selection of evidence. In order to protect a precious belief we concentrate on the arguments supporting it and neglect evidence that threatens it. We read the papers that advocate our views and uncritically accept information that supports our opinions. "The human intellect," wrote Bacon, "in those things that have once pleased it, brings everything else to support and agree with them; and, though the weight and number of contradictory instances be superior, still it either overlooks or despises them. And so he made a good answer, who, when he was shown hung up in the temple the votive tablets of those who had fulfilled their vows after escaping from shipwreck, and was pressed with the question, 'Did he not then recognize the will of the gods?' asked, in his turn, 'But where are the pictures of those who have perished, notwithstanding their vows?' " Our desire to preserve preconceived opinions makes us blind to facts, however abundant, that could be awkward, and encourages us to seize upon evidence, however scanty, that might prove useful.

Such partial selection of evidence, among other results, encourages people to find scapegoats. In

1914, for example, people maltreated dachshunds on account of their German origin. Many serious historical interpretations are equally ridiculous, mainly because so many people persist in turning to the past not to learn what it has to teach but to fortify their prejudices. The facts of history, like the letters of the alphabet, can be so arranged as to mean anything. By selecting convenient instances we may prove that the Jesuits or the Jews are responsible for all our troubles, that it is Freemasonry that makes the world go round, or that civilization is the record of undeviating progress, or regress, or what you will.

There are few more promising subjects for the study of prejudice than the color problem. The American colonists, having declared it "to be self-evident that all men are created equal," continued for nearly a century to legalize slavery. Millions of Negroes were kept in captivity while their masters proclaimed the principles of liberty and equality. This contradiction between precept and practice naturally troubled sensitive consciences, and the opponents of slavery were quick to point out the anomaly. Happily, the slave owners soon discovered that the phrase "all men" excluded Negroes, who were not, properly speaking, men at all, but a subspecies of man, intellectually and morally inferior to white people, and completely uneducable. They were children who grew old without growing up and therefore slavery was in their best interest.

A few obstinate eccentrics, however, persisted in challenging this racial theory, and so further arguments were brought forward in an attempt to convert them. The average Negro brain, it was found, was forty cubic centimeters smaller than that of a white person, and on the assumption that brain power and brain area are directly proportional, these measurements were alleged to establish the black man's inferiority. Of course, it would never have done to investigate this question of brain size too closely once it had served its purpose. Indeed those who persist in correlating intellectual capacity with skull capacity would almost certainly be the first to deny that Polynesians, Kaffirs, and Eskimos are superior to Europeans, although all have larger brains. To use an argument when it supports our preconceptions and reject it in another context when it fails to do so is known as "special pleading." During the last war the Red Cross segregated Negro and white blood for use in transfusions. The very people who dreaded the contamination of Negro blood, and hence Negro characteristics, raised no objection to being injected with serums derived from the blood of horses. They were indifferent to the danger of growing a tail but seriously alarmed by the prospect of having black children.

The fallacy of special pleading is exceedingly common. Discussions often take place in which at least one disputant tries to reap the benefit of an argument which he later pleads has a special reference to his own case but which somehow does not apply to others. Rich people sometimes argue against paying workingmen higher wages on the ground that they only waste money on beer and betting on horse races. Yet those who advance this argument are prepared to defend their own extravagances by claiming that they provide people with work. In fact, they believe in one argument for the rich and another for the poor.

Most of us think that we deserve a large salary because of the particular importance of the work we do, because our savings increase the wealth of the country, and because our expenditure maintains full employment; but equally most of us believe that the wages we pay other people should be low because the country cannot afford the burden of a vast wage bill, because hardship breeds independence, and because we cannot be expected to provide others with luxuries we deny ourselves. The mutual inconsistency of these propositions never becomes apparent because they are propounded in different contexts. The best way to combat special pleading is to compel the person resorting to it to admit the underlying assumption of his argument and then force him to apply his general principle to the particular case he has ignored.

Whenever we feel very strongly and fear that our prejudices may lead us astray, we should reduce our arguments to their essentials and then translate them into similar arguments about subjects that leave us indifferent. An even better method of depriving arguments of their emotional content is to use symbols. The following argument becomes a good deal less convincing when expressed briefly and in different terms. "Town-bred children never understand the country, even if they live in it in later life. They leave litter everywhere they go and never remember to shut gates behind them. The other day a cow from the next door farm was run over because it strayed on to the road, and the reason it did so was that somebody had not closed a gate. The person who left the gate open was obviously brought up in a slum." This argument suggests that as no townsman understands the country, anybody who does not understand the country must be a townsman. To put the same idea into other terms: no millionaires enjoy walking, so anybody who dislikes walking must be a millionaire. Put in this form the fallacy of the original statement becomes clear, for bad arguments, like strong poisons, are as easy to detect in concentrated doses as they are difficult to trace in dilution.

3

Thought and Language

It is possible to think without using words, but the subtlety of human thought owes nearly everything to language. Until an idea is translated into words it remains nebulous. Language crystallizes it. People, when thinking hard, often talk to themselves, and it has even been argued that all thought consists of a dialogue of the mind with itself. Soliloquies, of which dramatists were once so fond, may appear absurd, but in fact the only thing that makes them ridiculous is that the actors declaim their thoughts aloud. The process of holding a kind of debate with oneself is an ordinary enough way of solving problems. That this is so illustrates the dependence of thought on words. Language enables us to store memories, to communicate ideas, and to learn from the experience of others. The development of speech is possibly man's greatest single achievement, but it is easily abused. Correctly employed it ensures clarity; improperly used it encourages confusion. It would be almost impossible to exaggerate the number of errors in reasoning that spring from linguistic fallacies.

A surprising number of arguments arise from the failure of disputants to define the terms they use. They believe themselves to be debating questions of fact whereas the real issue is the significance to be ascribed to words. Heated discussions often occur because people attach different meanings to the same phrase. Whether rhubarb is a fruit or a vegetable appears at first sight to be a matter of fact. Certainly it is a question that has encouraged controversy. But when we analyze the problem, it turns out merely to be verbal. If we define a fruit as the part of a plant that encloses the seed, then rhubarb is clearly a stalk, not a fruit. But if we define fruit as something eaten with sugar after the main course of a meal, then rhubarb is a fruit. It just depends on what we mean by "fruit."

A great number of words are generally recognized as having a particular meaning, and no confusion occurs when they are used. Most English-speaking people probably attach the same significance to terms like "hydrogen," "sugar," or "island"—although even with words like these ambiguity can arise. However, wide divergencies in interpretation begin to appear when we use words such as "law," "nature," or "democracy."

The existence of a common vocabulary by no means implies that the same words convey the same meaning to different people. A word like "law" can easily lead to confusion because there are at least three senses in which the term can be understood. The commands of a state are referred to as its laws. Generalized statements of observed facts about the universe are called laws. Sometimes, tendencies on the part of people or things to behave in certain ways are also described as laws. Now there are several important differences of meaning in these definitions. The law of the land can be broken, and general tendencies can allow of exceptions, but a law of nature is immutable. One type of law is made by man, another only perceived by man. In one sense, law is arbitrary, in another, inevitable. Thus any proposition that contains the word "law" is probably open to several interpretations.

The term "nature" is even more ambiguous than "law." The Oxford Dictionary distinguishes several senses of the word. First, it can mean the attributes a thing possesses:

> Yet do I fear thy nature:
> It is too full o' the milk of human kindness.

Secondly, it can mean the state in which man was before society became organized. Thirdly, it can mean the supreme power behind the universe, and lastly, it can mean anything not made by man, such as the stars, the sea, animals and mountains. When people raise the cry, "Back to nature," they may mean that we are to abandon all the arts of civilization and return to a state of primitive savagery, they may be proposing that we should dwell in close communion with the countryside, they may desire us to avoid whatever is artificial, or they may even intend that we should submit ourselves to the will of the Creator. But until they define the word "nature" as they would like it to be understood in the context, their meaning will remain a matter of conjecture. Endless arguments have arisen between disputants who have failed to agree what they mean by "nature." One person advocates a return to nature, in the sense of abandoning synthetic foods and all the other artificialities of modern life, and another, regarding "nature" as implying the primitive state of man's existence, describes the idea of going back to it as a denial of everything for which civilization stands. If both parties stopped to define their terms they would possibly discover they were in agreement.

The scientist's vocabulary is very precise, indeed it is an essential part of his method to define his terms accurately. In his hands language becomes a keen-edged weapon and precision proves to be power. The vocabulary of politics on the other hand is ill-defined and ambiguous. Words like "imperialism," "communism," and "capitalism" convey very different ideas to different people. The trouble with such terms is that they try to say too much. It is asking rather a lot of a single symbol to represent a concept of great complexity and diversity. Consider, for example, the word "democracy." "To Englishmen, trained in the liberal tradition of some three hundred years, democracy implies the fundamentals of personal liberty—that the people, if they so desire, can change their government; that no individual can be imprisoned, executed, or exiled without public trial; that every citizen should have the right to express his own thoughts freely." But to the Russians "demokratichesky," as they call it, means something different. It implies a classless state in which the means of production are owned in common, in which supreme power is wielded by an oligarchy, and in which opinions are silenced and individual rights submerged. Recently both Russia and the West have accused each other of being undemocratic, but, of course, the point at issue is what the term means.

Lincoln defined democracy as government for the people, by the people, and of the people. If by democracy we just mean government for the people, it does not necessarily matter whether power is vested in elected representatives or not. Dictators are, after all, capable of governing in the interest of a majority, and sometimes one man who knows his own mind is more effective than an assembly of cantankerous individuals. But if we believe that the only way of achieving government *for* the people is to ensure that we have government *by* the people, representative government becomes an essential part of democracy. To say that the Russians are undemocratic is only to say that by refusing to allow free elections and a free expression of opinion they do not attach the same significance to the word "democracy" as we do. If we are really anxious to condemn the Russians, we should prefer facts to verbal quibbles. Instead of saying their system of government is undemocratic, which is only a matter of arbitrary definition, we would do better to give statistics of the number of slaves they employ, or the number of alleged traitors they have executed. Facts speak for themselves.

There are words which are not exactly ambiguous but whose meaning depends upon the context in which they are used. Such nouns and adjectives are described as "unfinished terms." To say, "Honesty is the best policy" is not to tell us whether it is best for honest people, or for those who have dealings with them, or for society in general. Political thinkers talk a lot about equality, but without further information the term means little. The Frenchman of 1789, who was prepared to sacrifice his life for equality, probably would have been at a loss to decide if it was equality of status, or equality of income, or equality before the law, or equality of opportunity for which he fought. But since people are often readier to die than they are to think, this need not surprise us. Other unfinished terms are quite meaningless by themselves, and so appeal to the lazy-minded who find it easier to say nothing in particular than to be explicit. Reviewers, for instance, frequently find books "suggestive," but what they suggest the reader has to decide for himself.

There are a great number of words that frustrate reasonable argument by stimulating emotions and prejudices. If one refers to a Negro as "a colored person" one merely states a fact, but if one calls him "a nigger" one suggests disapproval and contempt. The same quality may be described as faith or credulity depending upon our standpoint. The Christian, who is ready to congratulate himself on his faith in the Bible, may be equally prepared to deplore the credulous way in which Mohammedans trust the Koran. Words that imply emotional attitudes are described as "emotive," and the emotions they arouse are called "tied suggestions." The phrase "mob rule" suggests something disagreeable, whereas the tied suggestion attached to the term "democracy" is one of approval.

Obviously a language that had no vocabulary of praise or abuse would be an imperfect instrument with which to express thought. Emotionally toned words are invaluable to poets and orators. Without them the wings of fancy would be clipped. But clear thinking is baulked by strong feeling, and emotion is out of place in logical arguments. Writers and speakers often appeal to the heart and not to the head, confident that abuse or flattery will be more persuasive than reason. "Thus, 'a farsighted prophet' to his supporters is in the eyes of his opponents 'a crazy visionary'; a 'bold maneuver' becomes 'an impudent plot,' a 'new idea' is described as 'a newfangled notion,' a 'delicate hint' is turned into 'a subtle insinuation,' 'an ingenious plan' into 'a harebrained scheme.' "

Of course, some schemes are in fact "harebrained" and others are undoubtedly "ingenious," but when the merits and faults of a plan are being discussed, praise or insult is no substitute for argument. If a scheme is "harebrained," evidence should be produced to show why. Merely to call it "harebrained" is not to establish that it is so. Indeed by using the phrase "harebrained" in the course of discussion, we are assuming what we are endeavoring to prove. Our concern should be primarily with facts not words. If during court proceedings a prosecuting counsel described a prisoner as "an infamous wretch" he would at once be rebuked by the judge. The whole point of a trial is to establish by reasonable argument the guilt or innocence of the accused. To prejudge the issue is inadmissible. Calling a man a rogue does not make him one, although unfortunately, it may persuade people to regard him as one.

When we assume the point in dispute and take for granted the truth of something which requires to be proved before an argument can be accepted, we are said to "beg the question." We smuggle into a previous stage of the argument the conclusion about to be deduced. There is a well-known saying: "I am firm; thou art obstinate; he is pigheaded." Each of these phrases might be used to describe the same quality of steadfastness. Moreover, each phrase suggests an attitude to be taken toward such steadfastness. To be firm is to earn approval. To be pigheaded is to ask for censure. But whether a particular instance of steadfastness is admirable or despicable must be decided by evidence and argument, not by employing emotionally toned words implying condemnation or applause. To accuse somebody of being "pigheaded" is not to establish the charge, and unless evidence is produced the phrase merely begs the question.

The very extravagance of emotive language frequently betrays it for what it is. Only the simplest-minded reader could believe that Ruskin's attack on Whistler was addressed to reason. "I have heard and seen much of cockney impudence before now, but never expected to hear a coxcomb ask two hundred guineas for flinging a pot of paint in the public's face." This statement translated into factual rather than emotional language reads: "I never expected to hear a London artist charge two hundred guineas for his pictures." If Ruskin had contented himself with some such comment, the merit of Whistler's art, which was what was at issue, would have remained unsettled and the question would not have been begged. An effective way of getting rid of the logically irrelevant emotions associated with certain words is to substitute letters of the alphabet for them. "I have heard and seen much of C but never expected to hear W ask X guineas for P" is a less damaging contention than the original and one which it is easier to consider impartially.

Queen Victoria was very inclined to choose words which implied that the point at issue had already been settled. In her letters she considerately underlines some of the question-begging phrases so as to give them emphasis—perhaps on the principle that where the argument is weakest it is advisable to shout loudest. In a letter to her private secretary, Sir Henry Ponsonby, written in 1880, she says: "The Queen is *no* partisan and *never has* been since the first three or four years of her reign. But she has most *deeply* grieved over and been *indignant* at the *blind and destructive* course pursued by the opposition which would *ruin* the country."

The vocabulary of question-begging phrases is mercilessly exploited by politicians. There is no better time to observe such words at work than during election campaigns. The electorate likes to feel that it casts its votes after a rational consideration of the arguments put forward by rival parties. Consequently, political speakers make a pretense of appealing to reason, knowing, in fact, that the real vote-catchers are emotion and prejudice. At the English election of 1935 *Punch* advised candidates to remember the following useful phrases:

Your Side	The Other Side
Comprehensive program of reform	Unscrupulous electioneering manifesto
Trenchant criticism	Vulgar campaign of personal abuse
Shrewd thrust	Unmannerly interruption

These terms describe exactly the same objective facts, but the tied suggestions of approval or disapproval they contain make a great difference in the effect they have on audiences. To describe a party as a "faction," or a movement as an "agitation," to refer to a pledge as a "claim," or an appeal as a "bid," is to prejudge the issue.

Another form of question-begging is to argue in a circle. Theologians, for instance, sometimes try to prove the existence of God by referring to the evidence of the Old Testament. If the authority of the Bible is challenged they then defend it on the ground that the Scriptures are divinely inspired. The fallacy is admirably illustrated by Lewis Carroll. Alice, at one point in her travels in Wonderland, remarks that she has no desire to live among mad people. The Cheshire Cat tells her: "Oh, you can't help that, we're all mad here. I'm mad. You're mad." When she asks how he knows that she is mad, he replies: "You must be or you wouldn't have come here."

A statement such as "Chloroform makes one drowsy because it has soporific qualities" is technically known as a tautology. What, in effect, has been said is: "Drugs inducing sleep make one sleepy." Circular arguments become more plausible and less easy to recognize if developed at length, as the following example shows. "It is degrading for a man to live on a dole or any payment made to him without his being required to render some service in return. The reason is that he thus becomes, from an economic standpoint, a parasite upon the community as a whole, a position which is inconsistent with the maintenance of an individual's self-respect." In other words, it is degrading to accept unemployment pay without working for it, because to have unemployment pay without working for it is degrading.

A common practice of the question-begger is to preface statements requiring proof with such phrases as: "It cannot be denied that . . . ," "Nothing is more evident than . . . ," "It stands to reason that . . ." Macaulay was very fond of sentences beginning "Every schoolboy knows." The information this mythical child was alleged to possess would have discountenanced an encyclopedia. Questions may also be expressed in ways that partly anticipate their answers. The classic example is provided by the enquiry: "Have you left off beating your wife?" If only the answer "Yes" or "No" is allowed, by implication one admits the charge of wife-beating, whichever reply one gives. Clear thinking is impossible unless we use words which refer to facts and suspect those which express emotions. It is only reasonable to use emotive language in maintaining our views, provided we have not arrived at them by question-begging. "Words," as Hobbes once said, "are wise men's counters, they do but reckon by them, but they are the money of fools."

4

The Power of Suggestion

A man who spends a night in a reputedly haunted room is likely to be in a suggestible condition. He hears a rustle and peers into the darkness. A faint light moves by the window. Forgotten stories heard in childhood flood into his mind and he is seized with panic. "Every impression that comes to us from without," wrote William James, "no sooner enters our consciousness than it is drafted off, making connection with what is already in our mind." Vague shadows take on recognizable form, and the corner of a towel caught in the moonlight assumes human shape. The mind's tendency to fill in the blanks, without even knowing that it is doing so, leads to a great deal of inaccurate observation. In law courts people often give evidence which they honestly believe to be impartial, but which in fact has been distorted to fit in with their interpretation of events.

The creative activity of the mind in observation is illustrated by the fact that in reading santences we often fail to notice misprints which may appean. The correct beginnings of the words create the expectancy of a certain end and so we assume we have read letters which do not exist. Possibly on this principle you may have overlooked the two misprints in the sentence before last. Mr. Jepson in his book on *Clear Thinking* tells the following story. "I was present some years ago at a lecture by a professor of psychology. He began by talking to us about Napoleon's campaigns and referred to the battles of Marengo, Hohenlinden, Austerlitz, Jena, etc. Suddenly, without warning, he produced and showed for a second a piece of white cardboard with a word on it printed in large capitals. He asked us to write down the word we had seen. The majority of us wrote battle. As a matter of fact the word was bottle!"

Not only the interpretation of evidence, but the very principle on which it is selected and presented depends upon unconscious mental processes. If a man were asked how many legs the chair he was sitting on had, he would probably answer four, and if somebody then enquired how he knew, he would almost certainly reply that he had seen them. In fact without turning chairs upside down it is difficult to see all their legs at once, and what would be honestly described as "seeing" would actually be partly a matter of inference. Every observation we make must inevitably be interpreted in terms of our past experience and knowledge. We can never hope to see things as they are in themselves, since, in the very process of noticing them, our minds relate them to preconceived notions. It is impossible not to interpret experience without imposing upon it from the start ideas which are already in the mind, just as it is impossible for a man wearing blue-tinted spectacles not to see colors distorted.

Susceptibility to suggestion is one of the consequences of man's gregariousness. He tends to accept statements and opinions that are constantly repeated, whether there are grounds for believing them or not. The hypnotist who manages to send patients to sleep by telling them that they are becoming drowsier and drowsier, and the advertiser who persuades people to buy his wares because everybody else is doing so both rely on the power of suggestion. Our suggestibility involves us in a great deal of illogical thinking because it encourages us to accept ideas and opinions uncritically, without examining the evidence for or against them.

Human suggestibility arises from a deeply rooted instinct to respond to the herd. If several wolves are to maneuver as one, every wolf must instantly conform to the needs of the pack. The individual's sensitivity to such requirements is the essence of gregariousness. But man's instinctive desire to conform is fundamentally unreasonable, because it encourages him to accept as self-evident ideas prevalent in the community in which he happens to live. To accept such opinions without evidence, whether they be true or false, is irrational. The power of suggestion accounts for the efficacy of any argument which attempts to influence people by appealing to sentiments such as patriotism, group loyalty, and love of tradition (technically known as the "*argumentum ad populum*").

Print gives additional authority to suggestion because it bears the stamp of herd approval. Those who have goods to sell or opinions to disseminate constantly rely on people's pathetic faith in the printed word. "I saw it in the paper" is one of the commonest reasons given for believing some improbable half-truth. "In our day it would not be an unfair description of education to define it as the art which teaches men to be deceived by the printed word." Many newspapers and most advertisers try to induce us to accept opinions, not by offering us reasonable grounds for conviction, but by resorting to irrational tricks of suggestion.

People tend to believe statements without requiring argument or proof, especially if they are made again and again with sufficient confidence. "What I tell you three times is true," said the bellman in the *Hunting of the Snark*. Hitler, whose cynical abuse of propaganda has rarely been equaled, said that if propaganda was to be successful it must never appeal to reason but must confine itself to endless repetition of a few simple points. When we remember how seldom human behavior is rational, it no longer seems strange that people tend to believe what is repeatedly affirmed.

Advertisers who depend upon slogans such as: "Beer is best" or "Drink more milk" obviously would not spend thousands of dollars on mere exhortation unless they were confident that doing so increased consumption and hence their profits. The statement "Beer is best" is dogma, not argument. Moreover, it contains an unfinished term. What is beer best of, and for whom? Is it to be preferred to gasoline for engines, or is it better than water for drunkards? The appeal of such advertisements is not addressed to reason but to man's habit of accepting without question what he is told sufficiently often. Even in the present case you may have allowed yourself to be persuaded that what I say is true, not because my arguments are cogent, but because I have repeated myself and written with emphasis.

People are very much more suggestible if they are awed by the prestige of a speaker or writer. Advertisements for patent medicines love to quote letters of acclaim from doctors designated by impressive strings of qualifications. The public are then supposed to assume that remedies praised by physicians of such eminence must be effective. The mention of a title, it seems, is equally compelling. There is probably good reason to think that the Queen is in a position to command the best that money can buy and that therefore shops which hold Royal Appointments are worth a visit; yet to buy a brand of tooth paste because some impoverished dowager professes to use it, or to wear a sock because it bears the signature of a duke is to be dazzled by irrelevant glories. The merit of a sock lies in its color, durability, and comfort, and good socks will not become any better, nor bad socks any worse, if signed by every peer in the realm. As for the qualities of different tooth pastes, our friend F.A.C.S., M.D., D.D.S., is probably the best judge.

At first sight, it may appear to be sensible to buy one brand of gasoline rather than another because some expert recommends it. The ordinary motorist knows little of cars and rightly defers to those who spend their whole lives driving and maintaining them. But as gasoline companies are prepared to pay well-known people to recommend their products, advice thus given is suspect. The fact is that all brands of gasoline of equal octane value are much the same and nobody risks his immortal soul by asserting that one is the best. What is astonishing is the innocent, not to say gullible, way in which people accept such advice, as if it were utterly impartial. It never occurs to them that if a man is handsomely paid to say something it is only reasonable to be skeptical of what he says.

Prestige achieved in one sphere gives no authority in another. Scientists, who are entitled as such to respect when speaking on their own subject, should not be regarded as experts when discussing immortality or grace, unless, of course, they have separate credentials as theologians. Well-known baseball-players are unlikely to have much of value to say on education, and there is no particular need to attach importance to the views of famous jockeys on divorce. The principle of cobblers sticking to their last is, however, often forgotten, and people whose views deserve no respect, except in so far as they are sensible, are regarded as authorities even on subjects about which they obviously know nothing. Although our ignorance forces us to rely on experts and to take much of what they say on trust, it should always be remembered that they may well be wrong even when pronouncing on their own subjects.

Appeals to the prestige of some authority or other must always be treated with suspicion, because to accept opinions out of respect for great men, ancient customs, or recognized institutions is to dispense with evidence and proof. Anyway, intellectual progress demands skepticism not submission. An argument that avails itself of the deference due to authority (the *argumentum ad verecundiam*) is not necessarily unreasonable. There are circumstances in which we would drift hopelessly if we did not summon a pilot, in which ignorance and inadequacy force us to accept expert guidance. But it is exceedingly tempting to call for help when we do not really need it, thus saving ourselves trouble. Only in the last resort should we be prepared to believe things without other evidence than that of authority.

Advertisers have nearly perfected the art of persuasion and their methods show how insidious is the influence of suggestion. Very few advertisements appeal to reason, most prefer assertion and repetition. A survey of advertisements for whisky, taken from an old copy of a magazine, shows the sort of slogans that are found to be effective. One brand is described as "Scotland's best," another as "First because of its magnificent blend," and yet another as "The world's gentlest, most flavorful whisky imported from the world's oldest distillery." It might seem that the manufacturers of "the world's most flavorful whisky" were betrayed into making a damaging admission in referring to the antiquity of their distillery, were it not for the American public's affection for anything old. Other advertisements rely on flattery. "For people of inherent good taste," says one. "For those who appreciate the finest," says another. Finally, there is the whisky which claims that it is "Prized by connoisseurs the world over." All these advertisements have this in common: they depend upon unsubstantiated assertion and are designed to persuade by suggestion. As everybody's whisky is apparently the best, it is perhaps fortunate that the manufacturers deliberately avoid argument. Indeed, they probably do so only because they know quite well that unless they make their whisky cheaper, or better, there is no particular reason for drinking their brand rather than any other.

One of the most important functions of the gregarious instinct is to enable the pack to unite against danger. The herd's security often depends upon its sensitivity to its safety, and hence fear is perhaps the easiest suggestion to convey. If one sheep is frightened, the entire flock run, and the speed with which panic can spread through a crowd shows man's affinity with other animals. A considerable number of advertisers play upon fear and, indeed, create fear, because they realize how infectious it is. Clothes advertisements play upon the fear of being the odd man out, the strange creature whom the rest of the herd ignore or destroy. Incorrectness in dress, it is hinted, involves loss of caste or a betrayal of social ignorance. Manufacturers of medicine constantly exploit people's health fears and even invent diseases in order to increase their sales. It is, after all, easy to cure imaginary ills. The fear of growing fat has helped sell innumerable weighing machines, waist reducers, slimming pills, and diet booklets. One advertisement combines the fear of becoming corpulent with the fear of becoming repulsive. It consists of a picture of an enormously fat man sitting dejectedly at one end of a park seat. At the other end a boy and girl are embracing. The caption reads: "And this guy wonders why he is no devil with the ladies." Happily, the solution is simple. The fat man, it appears, has only to drink cabbage juice, or eat rusks, or something of that kind, to become bewilderingly attractive. Fear of going bald, fear of being excelled by our neighbors, and fear of being old-fashioned have all been used to stimulate prodigious expenditure. Indeed, creating a demand for products which few people need is part of the advertiser's art, and as there can be no good reason for buying what is worthless, the appeal is naturally not to thought but to feeling.

The technique of oratory resembles that of advertising, except that sometimes speakers have nothing to sell. If politicians tried to present the electorate with rational arguments, they would inspire little enthusiasm, because the matter of political thought is both extensive and dull. A speaker who began to explain even the premise of his argument would probably empty the hall, particularly as the reluctance of an audience to be instructed is usually proportional to its ignorance. Facts and statistics, the raw materials of proof, are difficult to master and harder still to make interesting. Consequently, speakers either avoid arguments altogether or produce them in so garbled a form as to be unworthy of the name. Politicians prefer to appeal to easily aroused emotions. The logical content of an ordinary election speech could almost certainly be summarized on the back of a postage stamp. It is deplorable that problems whose solution demand clear and impartial thought should be decided by frivolous and irrelevant emotions.

At the general election of 1931 Mr. Baldwin addressed a meeting at Leeds which opened his campaign in the north of England. The time was one of widespread unemployment. His solution of the problem was to form a National government consisting of Conservatives, Liberals, and such Labour members as could be persuaded to join. Here is part of his speech: "It is with the fullest confidence that I am starting my campaign in the industrial North. I put my faith in the good, sound common sense of Yorkshire men and women." In these first two sentences Mr. Baldwin puts his audience into a receptive mood. A speaker so quick to realize the merits of the Yorkshire character is obviously a man whose views deserve respect. "They are far too level-headed to be bamboozled by the crazy promises of the Socialists." Flattery of the audience is here combined with a question-begging denunciation of the other side. "Workers up and down the country are tired of parties which can do nothing but promise more and more doles when they know full well that the money is not in the till. What we want is a government which will honestly try to bring back work in the mines, the mills, and the workshops."

The suggestion is conveyed that the Socialists would attempt to solve the problem of unemployment by disreputable means, while Mr. Baldwin and his friends proposed to do nothing that was not aboveboard. "That is why they will give their support in overwhelming numbers to the National government." The audience is given to understand that this conclusion has been reached as a result of logical argument, whereas in fact it is mere assertion. Moreover, the statement suggests that to vote for the National government is to side with the majority, always a comfortable and reassuring thing to do. "When the financial storm arose and when the Labour government saw nothing but shipwreck ahead, shipwreck for itself and shipwreck for the country, had we been astute politicians we should have refused to co-operate in saving the ship. We should have made party capital out of the distress which had occurred to the nation and forced an election then and there." Mr. Baldwin gives the impression that his party is solely guided by patriotism, and that all who love their country should vote for him. Candidates at general elections have a policy to sell, and their methods are those of other advertisers. They flatter, they intimidate, they play upon herd instinct, and they arouse emotions of love, scorn, pity, and hatred. Apart from rebuking their opponents for inconsistency, their nearest approach to logical argument too often consists in empty appeals to reason. Mr. Baldwin doubtless won the confidence of the electors of Leeds. Certainly he knew what they wanted and gave it to them in full measure. But when the last cheers had died down and the audience had dispersed, some of them must have realized that a wagonload of rhetorical chaff is but a poor substitute for a grain of sense.

The most vicious attack made on reasonable thinking is that of the cheap daily papers, and the assault is no less formidable for being incidental to their main objective: to increase their circulation. The popular press began with Sir George Newnes' *Tit-Bits* and Lord Northcliffe's *Daily Mail.* The Education Acts of the late nineteenth century increased the size of the reading public, and newspapers like *The Times* and *The Morning Post* were far too serious to interest this new class of reader. Northcliffe, in particular, saw that a fortune could be made by giving the public what it wanted. Instead of fighting ignorance and prejudice and raising the tone of political discussion, he decided to publish a paper whose sale would be secured by getting down to the level of the half-educated reader. The schools now, he said, "are turning out hundreds of thousands of boys and girls annually who are anxious to read. They do not care for the ordinary newspaper but they will read anything which is simple and is sufficiently interesting." Northcliffe recognized exactly how the new sort of reader could be exploited: "There they are, millions of them" he argued, "waiting with pennies in their hands. Anyone can get those pennies who will give them what they want. Evidently the new readers do not want the old-fashioned newspapers. They cannot understand them and have not enough time to read them. They have not concentration enough to wade through their voluminous reports. Their minds demand scraps, tit-bits. Well, why not give them scraps? News can be treated in a way that will please them; make them feel they know all about everything, instead of suggesting to them, as existing newspapers did, that everything was very difficult to understand, that nothing could be discussed or reported except at great length."

Such were the auspices under which the popular press began and such is the tone it retains to this day. By its appeal to emotion and prejudice, by partial selection of evidence in its reporting, by pandering to the mental habits of its readers and by oversimplifying what is inherently complex, the cheap press encourages every sort of crooked thinking, and sets millions of people an example of which it should be ashamed. What makes matters worse is that a considerable number of newspaper owners, editors, and journalists know perfectly well what they are doing, and cynically defend their greedy corruption of the masses on the ridiculous plea that the public gets the papers it deserves.

The editor of a popular newspaper seldom dares to disturb his readers' cherished convictions, because by doing so he risks reducing his paper's circulation. Knowing how ready people are to allow passion to overrule their better judgment, and realizing how reluctant they are to be compelled to think, he finds it profitable to withhold unpleasant truths and to encourage comfortable falsehoods. "The effect, if not the avowed aim, of the popular newspapers, with their boasted circulations of over a million copies an issue, is no less an evil than the mass production and standardization of thought, culture, and taste at the lowest level."

The best way to avoid becoming a prey to suggestion is to recognize it, whatever disguise it assumes. Once it is unmasked it is no longer so dangerous. Whenever we find ourselves vigorously assenting to what we hear or read, we should be on guard, for it is a warning that we are in a highly suggestible mood. It is an excellent practice to regard any opinion that pleases us with suspicion and apply to it the critical standards we normally reserve for views we dislike. If we distrust our feelings, if we require evidence for our beliefs and if we cultivate skepticism, we should at least be able to counteract some of the ill effects arising from the irrational tendencies of our highly suggestible natures.

5

The Simple Truth

The world we live in is so complicated that the truth about it is unlikely to be simple. There are, of course, some facts which are quite straightforward, but then they are not usually questioned. The moment we begin to deal with anything controversial, the truth almost certainly ceases to be simple, even though it may still appear simple to those who feel strongly about what is disputed. Indeed, we are often tempted to impose an orderliness upon facts which exists only in our own minds. Few true statements about complicated matters can be expressed briefly, although many people believe that they have mastered a problem once they have eliminated qualifications, distinctions, and uncertainties. In this way Darwin's theory of evolution has been reduced to the simple formula: "Men are descended from monkeys," and Freud's psychological theory has been dismissed as the view that "everything is sex." As both men found it necessary to explain their ideas at great length, it is unlikely that these summaries do them justice; perhaps that is why they appeal most to opponents of their views.

The theory that the Germans were solely responsible for the first World War provides a good example of oversimplified thinking. The immediate occasion of the 1914 War was the assassination of the heir to the Austrian Empire. The murder was committed by a Bosnian student whose intentions were unknown to the Kaiser. This incident, of course, need never have involved Russia or France or any other of the great powers, but in the dangerous atmosphere of international politics then prevailing the spark set off an explosion. Germany was largely responsible for creating the conditions in which small disturbances involved widespread repercussions, but she cannot justly be blamed for everything that happened. The provocative and arrogant behavior of Serbia, which threatened to destroy the Hapsburg empire, Russia's support of Slav nationalism, France's burning resentment of her defeat in 1870, and Britain's resistance to German colonial and naval expansion all contributed to the final crisis. So complicated a situation as that which leads to a European war is unlikely to be explicable in a sentence, and agreeable as it is to make our enemies scapegoats for every disaster, it is a temptation we should try to resist.

Concise and epigrammatic statements have the practical advantage that they are readily remembered and easily diffused. Rousseau's doctrines would have had little influence if they had been confined to his writing. Few people are prepared to study books on political philosophy. Moreover, the great majority of Frenchmen in the eighteenth century could not even read. But they could understand and repeat a single slogan, and therefore, when the doctrine of Rousseau's "social contract" was summed up in the phrase "Liberty, equality, and fraternity," it instantly became the creed of thousands of revolutionaries.

Complicated policies are often presented to the electorate in the form of easily remembered catch phrases. These are comforting to repeat and they save the trouble of thinking. After the first World War the cry was "Hang the Kaiser," "Make the world safe for democracy," "Homes for heroes," and "Make Germany pay." Such slogans were not necessarily unreasonable. The electorate has to be influenced somehow, and politicians are not bound to bewilder their audiences by going into every argument. Provided slogans are used only to stir people to action and not as a substitute for thinking, it is legitimate to use them. But the phrase "Hang the Kaiser," for example, is not an argument, and to believe in the efficacy of the policy suggested just because it is repeatedly commended is no more reasonable than to buy a patent medicine merely because its manufacturers constantly claim that it cures everything from seasickness to malaria. "Canned thinking (like canned meat) is not dangerous provided that fresh thinking has preceded it."

We are often guilty of oversimplified thinking when we suppose that there is only one cause or one solution of a problem. The Nazis believed that if they exterminated the Jews their troubles would be over. Some people insist that England's prosperity depends upon returning to the gold standard. Others confidently assert that unemployment would be banished if the dole were abolished, or if jobs were made to go around by putting everybody on short shifts, or if the government provided work on the roads. As for the growth of juvenile delinquency, that presents no problem. It really all boils down to the fact that we are too soft with children today. What they really understand is a good thrashing. "Spare the rod and spoil the child." Such sweeping assertions may easily contain some truth, but not the whole truth, for the whole truth requires a consideration of all the facts, not a simplified version of a few of them. Some children are undoubtedly spoiled, but then others are sadly neglected, and there is little evidence to suggest that those who are spoiled are more likely to commit crimes than those who are neglected.

It is true that there are children who respond to no appeal other than fear, and the bully, who is at heart a coward, may well benefit from a dose of his own medicine; but to argue that indiscriminate flogging would always be effective is to ignore the fact that some boys are quite unmoved by it, and others out of daredevilry may even be encouraged to incur it. No punishment can possibly be suitable for all crimes and for all miscreants. Juvenile delinquency takes innumerable forms and springs from a number of different causes. The most that can reasonably be said of corporal punishment as a remedy is that it may be suitable in some cases for some crimes. So cautious and limited a proposition, however, appeals little to dogmatists, who believe that to have the courage of one's convictions, even where the evidence warrants nothing but skepticism, is a supreme intellectual virtue.

A trick very often used in controversy is to simplify the argument of the other side so that it becomes untenable. It is then much easier to refute. Nowadays it might be dangerous for anybody working on atomic physics to express the faintest sympathy with even one of the aspirations of communism. A scientist who did so would risk his job, particularly if he worked in America. It is quite reasonable to prevent vital technical information from falling into the hands of possible enemies, and as the Communists have declared their hostility to the capitalist West, we may well regard them as enemies. But because a man sympathizes with one particular Communist aim, that does not make him a Russian spy. Communism is a complicated creed which has something to say about most human activities, and, however perverse we believe its doctrines to be, we must admit that it is unlikely to be wrong about everything. Yet if a scientist were to say that the Communist doctrine of sharing all things in common was also held by the early Christian church, his words would possibly be exaggerated into a wholehearted panegyric of Russian communism.

The sort of man who sees everything as black or white, who despises half measures, who sweeps aside reservations, and who demands a straight answer to a straight question will always be ready to credit anyone who expresses the slightest sympathy for any aim of a political party with the most extreme views of its most advanced members. Such a person would immediately construe the statement that Mussolini made Italian trains run on time as a confession of faith in Fascism, and would regard an Englishman who expressed doubts about Britain's moral right to Malta or Gibraltar as a traitor anxious to sell his country to the highest bidder. It is seldom any good trying to point out to those who insist upon extending our arguments that they are being both unjust and illogical, because they would only reply that we are splitting hairs.

It would be wrong to think that the only people who extend our arguments are our opponents. In the heat of argument we may ourselves involuntarily exaggerate our case, or we may be lured into doing so by an adversary. Let us suppose, for example, that two men are arguing about the life of the English working class in the early part of the last century. The first maintains that the worker's lot was one of unmitigated misery; people were compelled to work eighteen hours a day for scanty wages, they lived in ghastly slums and, under the circumstances, were probably fortunate to starve, as so many of them did. The other argues that mechanization led to better pay and that although the industrial revolution had its growing pains, most goods became more widely available and much cheaper. As the argument proceeds, both disputants begin to make wild statements, until in the end one man is painting a rapturous picture of the idyllic existence of the working class in early Victorian England, while the other describes the conditions of factories and mines in terms reminiscent of the most horrifying passages of Dante's "Inferno." The arguments on both sides have become so exaggerated as to be exceedingly vulnerable; like overblown balloons, their fiber is weakened by extension, and the slightest puff suffices to make them burst. It is easy enough to defend the moderate assertion that the introduction of machinery did some harm and some good, but it is very hard to maintain the extreme view that it did nothing but harm, or nothing but good, because in this form the argument can be exploded by a single contrary instance. We have only to produce evidence proving that one family suffered from the factory system to disprove the thesis that industrialism was universally beneficial.

In wartime oversimplified thinking becomes almost a duty. Any belief that encourages people to fight strenuously is serviceable and any idea that lowers morale is objectionable. Ordinary men and women dislike war and find it easier to kill their fellows if they can regard them as barbarians. Thus, stories of enemy atrocities are enthusiastically circulated and accounts of their generous or humane behavior quickly suppressed. This oversimplified picture of the enemy is accepted not because it is true but because it is useful. Many people interpret history in the same spirit, ascribing every vice to one side and every virtue to the other. To some Protestant historians, Catholics at the time of the Reformation appear to be guilty of every conceivable crime. Such writers indignantly denounce the cruelty of the Inquisition, the bigotry of the Council of Trent, and the conspiracies of papists against Queen Elizabeth. On the other hand Catholic historians condemn with equal eloquence the cruelty of the Protestant persecution of Romanists, the bigotry of Calvinism, and the conspiracies of heretics against orthodox rulers.

Individuals receive the same treatment. Richard III is customarily dismissed as a cruel, oppressive, and tyrannical figure, unredeemed by a single compensating virtue, whereas Henry V is represented as a heroic, handsome, lovable king, the epitome of a patriot. Human beings are too diverse and complex in fact to fit into such rigid categories, and it defies experience to insist that anybody is entirely without fault or entirely without merit. Among other things, man is not sufficiently consistent. The murderers of Buchenwald meticulously fed starving birds during cold weather, a practice which in no way mitigated their foul crimes but which nevertheless shows that even the most evil of creatures are not utterly devoid of feeling. Complicated facts do not lend themselves to simple judgments.

There are several reasons for the attraction of oversimplified thinking. People who are cautious and tentative are likely to be unimpressive. Moderate statements and half measures seem to indicate weakness and indecision, while bold and forthright assertions suggest strength and vigor. Then there is the difficulty of understanding and explaining complex propositions. Most people are inclined to take the easy way out. Rather than wrestle with a problem, they prefer to give in before the bout even starts. It is partly mental idleness that enables us to believe that Richard III was a complete villain, or Henry V a perfect patriot. A dispassionate estimate of every facet of their characters would involve considerable effort, which explains our affection for less subtle judgments.

Finally, simple ideas are easily remembered, easily explained, and easily disseminated. People who wish to influence opinion, whether teachers, advertisers, or politicians, naturally have to adjust what they say to the intellectual level of their audience: the larger the audience the lower the level. The leading articles of newspapers like *The New York Times* or *New York Herald Tribune* are addressed to a fairly small number of quite well-informed people and hence discuss important problems in a reasonable manner. But the cheaper press, addressing itself to its millions of readers, can rarely afford to be judicious, moderate, or intelligent. So the man in the street gets his news reduced to its simplest elements, chopped up into brief paragraphs, which in their turn are condensed into headlines.

The process of generalizing is essential to thought, yet in a sense it involves oversimplification. It is a two-edged weapon. Legitimately used, it can achieve great intellectual victories; disaster follows its mishandling or abuse. It is important, then, to be able to distinguish between valid and invalid generalization. To generalize is to infer that what has been found true in all known cases is true of all cases, even including those which have not been observed. Of course, we can generalize without making this leap from the known to the unknown. If I say, "All my brothers are clever," I am generalizing, although the assertion is based upon knowledge of all individuals concerned.

Animals are capable of this kind of reasoning. Cows soon learn that to touch certain types of wire is painful and they modify their behavior accordingly; indeed, if they were unable to generalize, some of them would spend half their lives receiving shocks from electric fences. Animals probably achieve their generalizations by instinct rather than by logic. Nevertheless, to act on the principle that what has happened on all known occasions must in similar circumstances happen again is suspiciously like a rational inference. Charles Darwin's discovery that all white cats with blue eyes are deaf is an example of a more subtle generalization. His theory arose from a series of observations from which he ascertained that in every known case white cats with blue eyes were deaf. If he had contented himself with the results of his own observations and what he could discover about other observations, the most he could have said was that many white cats with blue eyes were deaf; but he was prepared to go beyond his own experience and make a statement claiming to be true of all blue-eyed, white cats, past, present and future.

The principle of reaching a conclusion about all entities of a certain type, based on observation of only some of them, is the basis of all scientific generalization. When Newton propounded his law of gravitation, he claimed that bodies always tend to gravitate toward each other with a force determined by their mass and their distance from each other. Obviously Newton's law goes beyond the possibility of experience, for no man could measure the gravitational forces of all celestial bodies. Not all generalizations, unfortunately, are as cautiously asserted or as carefully verified as those of physicists and biologists. Generalizations about racial qualities are often exceedingly wild. People who confidently maintain that Englishmen are unemotional, that Scotsmen are mean, and that Welshmen are liars not only exceed what it is possible to know, but affirm what is manifestly incredible. Hitler's murder of six million Jews was the gruesome consequence of rash generalization, for the principle behind this annihilation of a race was that all Jews were alike. The mention of the name of one Jew alone suffices to show that dissimilarities exist. Saint Paul was a Jew and his example is not generally imitated.

Some generalizations may not at first sight appear to be generalizations at all. Remarks like: "Most of Gladstone's first cabinet were peers," or "Eton has produced more prime ministers than any other school," or "Half the clergy are underpaid," seem not to assert any general principle because they do not make statements about all of the species concerned. But in fact such statements imply generalizations. Before we can assert that Eton has produced more prime ministers than any other school, we must know how many prime ministers other schools have produced. In fact knowledge of all schools is presupposed in this statement about one. Similarly, we must have all the clergy in mind to say that half of them live on a pittance.

Generalization provides one way of arriving at truth; deduction, which is the opposite of generalization, offers another. A generalization goes from particular cases to a general principle (a method of argument alternatively known as induction), whereas a deduction proceeds from universal laws to individual cases. Observation of all known animals has led to the generalization that those possessing horns and hoofs are noncarnivorous. If we now apply this general principle to a particular case, say that of the devil, we can deduce that he must be a vegetarian. When a lawyer attempts to establish the innocence of his client, his arguments are often deductive. He tries to interpret the law in such a way that when it is applied to the conduct of the accused nothing criminal appears. Deductive reasoning must start from a general principle from which the deduction is to be made, and proceed to a conclusion by way of some statement linking the particular case in question with the law which is to be applied to it. Thus the generalization "All fish are cold-blooded" suggests the deduction that whales are not fish, provided the connecting information that whales are not cold-blooded is given. The general principle and the connecting fact which every deduction requires, are called the "premises" of the argument, and all arguments which follow this pattern are referred to as syllogisms.

The most famous example of a syllogism was suggested by Aristotle. "All men are mortal. Socrates is a man. Therefore Socrates is mortal." The syllogism is a form of deductive reasoning in which a conclusion is inferred from the premises given. It is an argument which maintains that if the truth of given premises be accepted, certain conclusions follow, because it would be inconsistent with what has already been admitted for them not to do so. The structure of the syllogism can be studied without consideration of its meaning if we substitute letters for words. The argument proving that Socrates was mortal can be represented thus:

All M are P. S is M. Therefore S is P.

Formal logic is the study of the structure of deductive reasoning. Its method is to ignore the content of propositions and deal only with their logical form. In order to do this it has established a symbolism of its own, avoiding the ambiguity and irregularity of ordinary language.

Logicians have identified two hundred and fifty-six variations of the syllogism and have distinguished the valid from the invalid. The reader would possibly find it wearisome to analyze them all! Fortunately, it suffices to examine only one very common and characteristic error, known as the fallacy of the undistributed middle, of which the following is an example. "All Fords are cars. I own a car. Therefore I own a Ford." The argument is invalid because although *all* Fords are cars, not all *cars* are necessarily Fords. The assertion "I own a car" does not logically imply that the car I own is a Ford. It might be, or it might not be.

One method of detecting logical fallacies is to concentrate on the form of arguments rather than on their content. It is always advisable to avoid judging the soundness of arguments by considering whether we agree with their conclusions. Since strong feelings weaken our critical sense it helps to translate arguments into a skeleton form. Nobody can fail to see what is wrong with the argument: All M are P, S is P, therefore S is M; but the fallacy may easily pass unnoticed when the same sort of reasoning is expanded into a paragraph, particularly if the subject concerned arouses our prejudices.

Generalization lends itself to crooked thinking even more readily than does deduction. It is in the nature of most generalizations to reach conclusions without complete evidence. The proposition that "All men are mortal," in so far as it covers human beings yet unborn, goes beyond the available evidence and asserts what cannot be known with final certainty. It is impossible to obtain exhaustive data in forming generalizations about human affairs. Such a statement as: "Red-haired people are hot-tempered," cannot be substantiated by a survey of every red-headed human being that ever existed. But although generalizations rarely take all evidence into account, sound ones have to satisfy certain important conditions.

The essential condition of a valid generalization is that it should derive from a sufficient number of representative instances. People are far too inclined to base general conclusions on isolated and possibly untypical experiences. The story is told of a New Zealander paying a first visit to England. No sooner had he landed at Southampton than a gust of wind blew some grit into his eye. "Well," he remarked, "it certainly is a very dusty country." Often, people condemn a whole profession because of the unfortunate conduct of a few of its members. "Another attorney sent to prison," they say. "It just shows that lawyers can never be trusted."

Valid generalizations must be based on fair samples, not carefully selected instances. Advertisers often print grateful letters from people who have bought their wares, and there is no reason why the evidence of a firm's mail bag should not provide a valid argument for buying its products. If thousands of purchasers are genuinely satisfied and only a few dissatisfied, it is extremely probable that the article in question provides good value. It is, however, essential to know if the letters selected for publication in the newspapers are typical of the majority of letters received. An unscrupulous firm might get ninety-nine letters complaining that its goods were worthless and that its claims for them were fraudulent, and only one letter praising its produce. If it then published the one and suppressed the ninety-nine, any generalization about the value or popularity of the firm's manufactures would be worthless, because it would be based on a carefully selected and uncharacteristic sample. To attack the Socialist Party for trying to undermine family life because one hot-headed member of it advocates easier divorce, or to accuse the Conservatives of desiring unemployment because some backwoodsman has said that hunger is the best incentive to work is to be guilty of selecting insufficient and unrepresentative evidence from which to generalize.

As the real motive of argument is often only to reinforce prejudice, we are inclined to seize upon facts which are agreeable to us and to ignore those which prove inconvenient. There is, therefore, a psychological provocation to generalize from partially selected facts. If we are to argue reasonably, we must counteract this tendency by searching for conflicting evidence. The confidence which we can repose in a generalization such as: "Dreams often come true," should not depend so much upon a few striking examples apparently verifying the statement, as upon the thoroughness of the search made for instances disproving the theory. Generalizations must be based upon investigations covering a sufficiently wide field, the instances from which they are derived must be representative, and even if they satisfy all these conditions, they should be regarded merely as a working hypothesis subject to constant review and revision.

When in the course of argument a generalization is attacked and evidence is produced of a particular case which does not obey the general principle in dispute, the defense is often put forward that such an instance is "the exception that proves the rule." This may silence criticism but it is a meaningless assertion. General rules admit of no exceptions, and if exceptions exist, all they prove is that the rule is false. The word "prove" in this saying originally meant "test" and, of course, the proposition that the way to test a general rule is to look for exceptions to it is very sound. It is possible that the assertion "The exception proves the rule" originated from a poor translation of the Latin phrase "*Exceptio probat regulam,*" which means that rules cover every case not especially excepted.

A great deal of confusion of thought arises because people fail to distinguish between "all" and "some." The nurse who told her young charge, "Nobody eats soup with a fork," and got the answer, "I do, and I am somebody," failed to qualify the term "nobody," and for that reason was refuted. Many statements imply "all" where only "some" applies. The slogan "Beer is good for you" suggests that all beer is always good for you, which is untrue if you are trying to slim, or if the beer has gone bad, or if you have drunk too much already. Many proverbs are typical half-truths which require qualification. "More haste less speed" is in some circumstances excellent advice, but it is not a principle one would advocate for a runner attempting the four-minute mile. But then as one of Dickens's characters says: "The bearings of the observation lays in the application of it."

6

Argument by Analogy

A very common error in argument is the assumption that because one thing follows another the second event must be the consequence of the first. This is the fallacy of "*Post hoc, propter hoc*": this came after that, and therefore this must have happened because of that. If thirteen people attended a dinner and a month later one of them died, superstitious people would attribute the fatality to the number thirteen. John Stuart Mill tells how the villagers of Tenterden attributed the formation of local quicksands to the building of a nearby church steeple. Before the steeple of the church was built there had been no quicksands. Soon after its erection, quicksands appeared. "Therefore," argued the inhabitants, "the one caused the other." Politicians are often very ready to point out that economic depressions that occur while they are in office are attributable to the adverse balance of world trade and have no connection whatever with their policy or administration, but the moment their opponents come into power everything which goes wrong is ascribed directly to the government's incompetence.

When we find two conditions existing side by side, it is tempting to conclude that one explains the other. There may, of course, be a necessary connection between the two things; but before the relation of cause and effect is established, it must be shown that if the effect did not follow the cause, some accepted general principle would be violated. Bernard Shaw was both a vegetarian and a brilliant playwright, but it does not follow that being a vegetarian in any way accounts for his excellence as a dramatist. No law of nature is defied by assuming that abstaining from meat is not the cause of writing great plays.

In the same way, a politician who wishes to gain the credit for some measure his party has inaugurated must show that the improvements which he maintains have followed its introduction would not anyway have taken place without legislation. Doctors as well as politicians find the fallacy of "*Post hoc, propter hoc*" flattering to their reputations. They make a diagnosis, prescribe a course of treatment, and the patient's symptoms disappear. The mere fact that some medicine was taken and a cure ensued proves nothing except that one thing followed the other. The medicine might easily have been utterly useless and the patient's recovery due entirely to the natural recuperative power of the body.

Historians are inclined to relate events by asserting that one caused the other, when the most that can reasonably be asserted is that they followed one another. The prosperity of mid-Victorian England is frequently ascribed to the establishment of free trade. Certainly, in point of time one thing followed the other, but the wealth of England in the eighteen-fifties might equally be attributed to the building of the railways in the previous decade, or to the development of the factory system, or the backwardness of other competitors, or to Britain's imperial markets, or to the size of her merchant navy. Free trade may have been the cause, or at least one cause, of Britain's industrial supremacy, but this is not proved by showing that one followed the other. We must further demonstrate the necessary connection existing between the two. As Germany's economic success after 1870 is often attributed to her policy of state control, there is reason to doubt that prosperity is only achieved by free trade.

The fallacy of "*Post hoc, propter hoc*" often coincides with the mistake of generalizing from selected instances. The belief that a man's death was in a sense caused by his being thirteenth at dinner involves neglecting a mass of evidence. It ignores the thousands of dinner parties of thirteen which have not been followed by the death of one of the guests. It overlooks the probability that of a dozen or so people one is anyway likely to suffer some misfortune within twelve months in the ordinary course of events. It disregards the fact that immediate causes like disease, old age, or accident provide a more convincing explanation of a man's death than do remote contingencies, such as the number of people who dined with him a year before. By selecting only those facts that substantiate a superstition and by neglecting those which fail to confirm it, we are able to prove almost anything. A man visits Naples and two years afterward dies; therefore his death was caused by seeing Naples. Provided we ignore the fact that he died by falling out of a window, provided we forget that he had visited Naples a number of times before without dying, and provided we never consider the extraordinary improbability of the alleged cause of death, it is possible to believe such nonsense.

Another type of reasoning that is often vitiated by partial selection of evidence is argument by analogy. Analogy forms the basis of much of our thinking. We see that two cases resemble each other in certain respects, and we consequently conclude that further similarities exist. The following extract from a letter to a newspaper provides an example of an invalid argument by analogy. "During this century Britain's aggressors have shared one sinister similarity: they have all spelled their names with six letters and all have the same second syllable. Thus: Krug-er, Kais-er, Hitl-er, and Nass-er. Maybe we should have spotted this before we let the last one get so far."

Analogy can be expressed as the argument that because X has the properties *a* and *b*, and Y has the properties *a* and *b*, Y must also have the property *c* which belongs to X. Arguments by analogy are not always immediately recognizable as such. Certain words and phrases imply them without asserting them. Thought abounds in metaphors, similes, and parables, and these often involve disguised arguments from analogy. For example, the assertion "The keen edge of the reader's intellect will be sharpened by studying logic," could imply the argument that the mind is like a weapon, which improves with use, and because studying logic involves strenuous thinking, it therefore improves the mind. The fallacy in the argument is that it entirely depends upon an arbitrary metaphor. Most weapons become blunted when used, and if the intellect is likened to a weapon of this sort the conclusion must be drawn that logic engenders feeble-mindedness.

Argument by analogy is extremely useful in persuading people to see situations in new lights by transferring arguments from subjects that provoke strong feelings to roughly similar topics that arouse no emotion. A fine example of this use of analogy is to be found in the second Book of Samuel. David, desiring Uriah's wife, put Uriah in the forefront of the battle to make sure he was killed. When the plan succeeded David married Uriah's widow. "But the thing that David had done displeased the Lord. And the Lord sent Nathan unto David. And he came unto him, and said unto him: There were two men in one city; the one rich, and the other poor. The rich man had exceeding many flocks and herds: But the poor man had nothing save one little ewe lamb, which he had bought and nourished up: and it grew up together with him, and with his children; it did eat of his own meat, and drank of his own cup, and lay in his bosom, and was unto him as a daughter. And there came a traveller unto the rich man, and he spared to take of his own flock and of his own herd, to dress for the wayfaring man that was come unto him; but took the poor man's lamb and dressed it for the man that was come to him.

"And David's anger was greatly kindled against the man; and he said to Nathan, As the Lord liveth, the man that hath done this thing shall surely die: And he shall restore the lamb fourfold, because he did this thing, and because he had no pity.

"And Nathan said to David, 'Thou art the man.'"

David, not recognizing that the case was his own, was able to judge the action of the rich man without special pleading. His instinct of self-justification was caught unaware. Consequently, when he was told "Thou art the man" the force of the argument proved irresistible. "And David said unto Nathan, I have sinned against the Lord."

Analogy, unfortunately, is not always a good guide. Foreigners may easily be led astray when learning English by relying upon comparisons. Because "mice" is the plural of "mouse," they expect "hice" to be the plural of "house," and because "slough" is pronounced so as to rhyme with "cow," they assume that "rough," and "dough," and "through" are all pronounced the same. The trouble is that things alike in some respects may differ in others. Whales resemble fish in that they live in the sea, but they differ from fish in giving suck to their young. All words ending in "ough" are spelled alike, but that does not mean that they are pronounced alike. We have to distinguish between similarities that are accidental and similarities that are necessary and inevitable. It is purely fortuitous that the first letter of the surname of all anesthetists I know happens to be P. As there is no general law which requires them to be called Pots, Philips, or Partington, it would be a mistake to argue that anesthetists cannot be called Simpson or Snow.

No valid analogy can be based upon a comparison of accidental similarities. A ship's engines and its engineer may both come from Glasgow, but that does not mean that the engineer requires oiling. On the other hand, it would be perfectly reasonable to argue that just as an engine will gradually stop working if it is starved of fuel, so the human machine will cease to function if it is deprived of food. Provided the analogy is pressed no further, the comparison holds good. Engines and human bodies both require fuel to produce energy, and in both instances the same consequence, ceasing to function, ensues from the same cause, cessation of fuel. It would not, however, be reasonable to argue further that as a machine can be restarted after months of inactivity if it is given the fuel it requires, so a corpse can be revived several months after death by being offered nourishing food. The analogy breaks down because a machine is not dead when it stops. If it were, it could never start again, death being irreversible. In so far as machines and bodies are similar, what is true of one will be true of the other. But in so far as they are dissimilar, and their differences are far more numerous, important, and striking than their resemblances, what applies to one is unlikely to apply to the other.

All analogies, if pushed too far, ultimately break down, while some arguments by analogy hardly even begin. In 1932, Mr. Baldwin broadcast to Britain because part of the cabinet had resigned. His purpose was to revive confidence in the National government. No doubt there were excellent reasons for continuing to support Mr. Baldwin, but whatever these were they did not appear in his speech. The argument, if it can be called an argument, which he put to his listeners, was as follows: "A little over a year ago, the ship of state was heading for the rocks. The skipper had to change his course suddenly, and many of his officers and most of his crew deserted. It was a case of all hands to the pumps, and I signed on with my friends, not for six months or a year; I signed on for the duration, be the weather fair or foul, and I am going to stick to the ship, whether it goes to the bottom or gets into port." What this in effect meant was that Mr. Baldwin was prepared to carry on the government at a time of crisis, despite the resignation of those who disagreed with his policy.

The nautical exploit described is certainly remarkable. The crew appears to have been engaged in mid-ocean upon very unusual terms. Moreover it is far from clear why they were required to man the pumps after the ship of state had avoided the rocks for which it was heading. But these are only minor criticisms. The whole logical force of the analogy depends upon the soundness of the comparison between the position of the government and the position of the officers and crew of a ship. It is not sufficient merely to assert that the cases are parallel, they must be shown to be parallel. In fact important differences exist. The officers of a ship are obliged to obey the captain's orders; to fail to comply with them is mutiny; but cabinet ministers can wrangle with the prime minister and, if necessary, resign. When a ship is sinking, there is probably only one effective preventive, but there may be several possible remedies for saving a nation in time of crisis, each with its respective merits and drawbacks.

Mr. Baldwin first attempted to persuade his listeners to accept his solution of the country's problems by presenting them with a very much simpler problem which admitted of only one solution, that is to say the problem of saving a ship. Then he went on to assert that the nation's crisis was essentially similar and consequently soluble by the same methods. Exactly what these methods were he never actually specified, but phrases like "signing on for the duration" and "sticking to the ship" sufficed to guarantee their soundness. We should always be on our guard against arbitrary analogies, which simply assert similarities without otherwise establishing them and which encourage us to accept solutions to complicated dilemmas by comparing them with simple problems which they only casually resemble.

No sensible person would wish for a captain who deserted his ship the moment danger threatened, but the ready assent we give to this exceedingly reasonable statement should not be transferred to other more dubious propositions. It should not, for example, have been regarded as a reason for accepting Mr. Baldwin's policy, any more than the argument that it would be absurd to allow a blind man to steer a ship should have led people to abandon him. Of course it would be ridiculous to choose a blind navigator, just as it would have been absurd to have voted for Mr. Baldwin if he lacked all political vision. But the question the Prime Minister's audience had to decide was whether Mr. Baldwin was in fact perceptive, and no amount of stories about steadfast captains and flighty crews could help them to do that. Only the evidence of a man's record enables us to assess his perspicacity.

Historical analogies are exceedingly common and frequently fallacious. To turn to the past to discover lessons to apply to the present is an irresistible temptation. The trouble is that history seldom repeats itself exactly, despite the maxim to the contrary. The similarity between two situations may be striking yet superficial, and the differences between them less apparent but more significant. Apes resemble human beings in many ways, but most people regard the distinction between men and monkeys as more important than similarities that exist. Charles I argued that the history of Queen Elizabeth's reign showed that England thrived under despotic rule, so he concluded that if his own government was to be successful he must check the growing power of the House of Commons. Even if we grant the very doubtful proposition that the achievements of the Elizabethan era were the fruits of tyranny, an argument, incidentally, which involves the fallacy of "*Post hoc, propter hoc*," it does not follow that expedients suitable to the Tudor age necessarily applied to the England of the Stuarts.

A plant which flourishes in one soil may wilt in another. In the same way forms of government cannot be transplanted without risk. Measures agreeable in one set of circumstances may only be aggravating in another. The Tudor despotism was welcomed because England was beset by perils that only strong government could avert, and the acquiescence of Elizabeth's subjects was not proof of their servility but of their willing acceptance of dictatorship. By 1625, circumstances had changed. The Spanish fleet had been defeated, the Protestant religion was firmly established in England, the danger of a disputed succession had passed, and Scotland was no longer hostile. The period of crisis was over. In these altered circumstances measures which had been welcomed in the Tudor age now seemed repressive and superfluous. Unfortunately, Charles I failed to recognize that times had changed, and the mistake cost him his life. The similarities between the England of 1588 and the England of 1625 were obviously considerable, but before arguing by analogy from such resemblances, Charles I should have paid greater attention to the growing differences which existed. It is just at the point where distinctions appear that analogies break down.

The historian who searches the past to discover remedies for present ills may easily make the same sort of mistake as Charles I did, particularly because his selection of evidence is likely to be determined by preconceived theories. Measures which once proved successful succeed again only if circumstances are identical. The tactics employed at Agincourt triumphed, but that does not mean that they would be applicable to modern war. Few present-day generals would seriously consider applying them, because the difference between fighting now and fighting then is so considerable. Nevertheless, the mistake of pursuing an outmoded strategy is exceedingly easy to make.

The French in 1940 tried to fight as they fought in 1914. They assumed that the methods which had enabled them to win the first World War would succeed a second time. But the Germans, dissatisfied with the tactics of a war which ended in their defeat, naturally enough decided to try something different. In 1940, their new technique proved overwhelming. The French had gone wrong because they failed to realize where the argument by analogy broke down. There were many deceptive similarities between 1914 and 1940. On both occasions the battles began over much the same ground. In both instances the Germans were fighting against France and England. Each time the attack came through the Low Countries. But the all-important distinction was that the Germans had conscientiously devised a new type of warfare, and the situation was therefore in that respect different. Any argument which failed to take this change into account suffered from the disastrous defect of pushing an analogy to its illogical conclusion. The theory that "History repeats itself" is profoundly unhistorical if it is regarded as anything more than a rough generalization, because by concentrating on similarities it overlooks changes. Nearly any thesis may be sustained by some parallel or other, and consequently arguments based on historical analogy are, at the best, to be handled with extreme caution.

Although there is often scanty ground for accepting arguments by analogy, such arguments nevertheless tend to produce conviction in the same irrational way as do slogans. Most people will accept a vivid argument by analogy without questioning the alleged similarity between the things compared. Moreover, many analogies have no logical force whatever and depend for their effectiveness upon stimulating the imagination. The Conservative speaker who accused the Liberal leader of sailing as near to the Socialist wind as he could without upsetting his frail craft doubtless persuaded some of his audience of the danger of supporting so reckless a helmsman, although any seaman would see at once that the metaphor was ludicrously inept, because the closer boats sail to the wind the less likely they are to capsize.

The statement "contains no grounds beyond mere assertion for the suggestion that it was the policy of the Liberals to be as socialistic as possible; but this assertion, being thrown into the form of a metaphor implying an analogy, is liable to carry more conviction than the bare verbal statement. The picture of the Liberal leader timorously edging his boat as close to the wind as he dares, sticks in the mind persistently and is accepted readily." Uncritical acceptance of imperfect analogies derives in part from mental laziness. If people were not so resistant to hard thinking, they would realize how often the analogies that encourage them to accept propositions could equally well be used to establish opposite conclusions. The Liberal leader, in the instance mentioned above, might have flung the sailing metaphor back at his Conservative opponent. Tories, he could have retorted, timidly remained in port when the weather looked threatening, whereas he ventured out to sea, despite the storm, and by steering close to the wind skillfully survived the tempest.

The economic slump that swept Britain in 1930 raised a formidable unemployment problem, and many people at the time believed that the emergency could best be parried by a coalition of all parties. They maintained that old scores ought to be forgotten, and that Conservative, Labour, and Liberal supporters should co-operate to end the crisis. "The truth is," said one such advocate of a National government, "that the ship is on fire. I am not disposed to enter into any controversy on the name of the pump that is to be used or the length of the hose. The main thing is that we should save the ship, and I have no doubt we shall do it." If we analyze the impact of this analogy upon an audience, it presumably has some such effect as the following: "The ship is on fire," declares the speaker. "Something must be done immediately," respond the audience. "To enter into controversy on the name of the pump that is to be used, or on the length of the hose would be to waste time." The audience assent. Naturally, they feel, names do not matter at such a time. Of course, the exact length of the hose is of small consequence. The vital need is to save the ship and not squabble over nice distinctions. "The main thing is that we should save the ship," concludes the speaker "and I have no doubt that we shall do it." "How lucky we are to listen to somebody who sees things so clearly," says the audience to itself, "and how thankful we should be to leave him and his supporters to save the situation."

Despite the dangers arising from analogy, it would be wrong to conclude that it is always unfruitful. Darwin was led to the theory of the origin of species by comparing natural selection as practiced by breeders and the methods whereby animals survive in the wild state. Analogy is a valuable guide to what we may expect to find, so long as the conclusions it suggests are regarded as tentative until otherwise confirmed. Analogy also provides an important means of exposition whereby notions outside our experience may be explained by comparison with familiar concepts. By itself analogy can prove nothing. Newton's achievement did not consist only of noticing the resemblance between celestial movements and falling apples, he had also to devise experiments and discover evidence to substantiate his theory of gravity.

The analogy alone would only have provided a brilliant hypothesis, whereas what Newton finally announced was a law of nature whose operation the whole universe confirmed. "Comparison should never be used as the sole support of a theory or judgment. It can be used by way of illustration and explanation, to elucidate or to verify a fact already established. It also has another very valuable use; it can often start a train of thought or suggest a working hypothesis." But it can do no more than this and should be forced no further. That it may easily become a snare was recognized by Samuel Butler when he prayed, "to be preserved from the evil one and from analogy."

Clear thinking is vitiated not only by fallacious arguments but by failure to stick to the point. It is the mark of the confused thinker that he wanders hither and thither and is easily distracted by irrelevant issues. A discussion that begins by considering the claim of papal infallibility is only too likely to degenerate into a squabble about the misgovernment of Rome in the early nineteenth century or the inability of Protestants to decide what they believe. Disputes that begin with factual problems, such as who has the best claim to a seat in a train, often go through a phase in which personal abuse of a totally irrelevant kind plays an important part. This diversion is known as the *argumentum ad hominem*. The contention, for instance, that a person who occupies a reserved seat is a bounder, apart from begging the question, is irrelevant to the point in dispute, namely whether the seat is, or is not, reserved. After all, bounders are perfectly capable of sitting on unreserved seats, while persons of impeccable breeding might through absent-mindedness or shortsightedness unwittingly occupy places which had already been taken.

Another form of diversion is to refute some trivial point of an opponent's argument and then suggest that his whole position has consequently been undermined. It is quite possible to give the impression that a contention has been discredited by fastening on some incorrect fact referred to in support of it but upon which it is not actually dependent. If a man were to declare that he doubted the literal accuracy of the Bible because he found it impossible to believe the story of Jonah and the whale, it would be true but irrelevant to object that the creature mentioned in the Old Testament is described as "a great fish." Hecklers rely on humorous objections to discredit speakers whose policies they oppose. Thus a politician who says in reference to overcrowding in slums that there are thousands of families living in rooms in which it would be impossible to swing a cat is not really refuted by the interrupter who shouts: "Then they shouldn't keep a cat." Although such a comment does not even contain the hint of a logical argument, it tends to make the speaker look absurd and puts him out of his stride. To reply to a heckler is to be diverted from the point, while to ignore him may leave the impression that his challenge is unanswerable.

There are a number of technical terms used to classify various ways of ignoring the point. We have already examined the *argumentum ad hominem* and the *argumentum ad verecundiam*. The first is summed up in a lawyer's advice: "No case: abuse plaintiff's attorney." The second is exemplified in the following statement: "As the author of a dozen or so books on psychology, perhaps I can claim to be qualified to diagnose a straightforward case of hysteria." Three other tactics of diversion are worth mention. First, the *argumentum ad ignorantiam,* which attempts to prove a proposition by asserting that it has never been disproved. Ghosts must exist because nobody has established that they do not. Secondly, the *argumentum ad populum,* which appeals to the herd instinct. "It's not American." "It's just not done." "It's not playing the game." Such phrases serve to distract attention from the real point at issue: the merits or defects of some proposed scheme. It may not "be American," for example, to work as hard as Germans work, but whether it is American or not has nothing to do with whether it is desirable. Finally, there is the *argumentum ad baculum,* the appeal to force, used by reasonable people in the last resort and by most of mankind at the earliest opportunity. Violence is no substitute for reason and a bloody nose is not an argument.

After the warning given above of the dangers of

analogy, it is possibly unwise to conclude with one, but the temptation is too strong to be resisted. A book on logic may be likened to a chart that indicates the shoals and rocks that ships must avoid. We can, if we like, try to navigate without one, allowing our instinct to guide us and trust in providence. We can dispense with the navigational assistance that maps provide, we can sail the seven seas not knowing the meaning of lights or the whereabouts of buoys, ignorant alike of tides, currents, and prevailing winds. But, naturally, if we are guided by instinct alone we shall be lucky to get within miles of our destination. Indeed, we are unlikely to arrive at all. Learning to navigate is certainly hard work. Nevertheless, if we wish to set a straight course, it is something we should know about. Those who would seek truth wherever it is to be found must train for the task, study the best maps available, and examine the dangers involved in order to avoid them. This book is a simple chart to clear thinking and the reader who decides to throw it overboard is wished good luck on his voyage. He will certainly need it.

APPENDIX A

The Good Old Days

The following extract from the minutes of the Great Muddle Debating Society provides the reader with instances of most of the errors mentioned in the text. An analysis of these fallacies will be found on page 114.

The Great Muddle Debating Society of England met recently to discuss the motion: "This house regrets the passing of the good old days." The chairman called upon Major Bigot to propose. The Major began by describing England's position a few years before the turn of the century. "In those days," he said, "we possessed the greatest empire ever known. Our navy was twice as large as that of any other nation and we were by far the richest country in the world. Today, the position is not so happy. Our overseas possessions have been squandered by a rabble of fanatical bolshies . . ." At this point Mr. Promise asked the chairman whether it was in order to refer to a group of enlightened statesmen, who had freed the subject races of Asia from the ignominious yoke of imperialist rule in the disparaging terms employed by the proposer. After some hesitation, the chairman decided that the words complained of were permissible. "Our navy," continued the Major, "is nothing more than an appendage to the American fleet, and our budgets are balanced only by going to the United States, cap in hand, and begging for dollar loans.

"Nobody in his right mind can deny that England was a very much better country to live in fifty years ago than it is today. That the last half century has witnessed a sad decline in manners and enterprise is unfortunately self-evident. Speaking as an army officer with some small experience of men, I do not hesitate to say that modern soldiers are mentally, physically, and morally inferior to the troops I commanded as a young subaltern during the first World War. The difference is one of upbringing. Parents today allow their children to do whatever they like. Boys of fourteen are allowed to smoke and drink. The rod is spared and the child is spoiled. Juvenile delinquency would cease to be a serious problem if magistrates were authorized to sentence young offenders to birching. I well remember a boy whom I employed shortly after the first World War telling me that a flogging he received for stealing apples had given him a lesson he would never forget. It just goes to show that a good hiding is the only thing boys understand.

"Unfortunately, nowadays, we have discarded the precepts of Solomon and seem to prefer the wisdom of Professor Freud. It is my considered opinion that no man is more to blame for our present difficulties than the so-called 'father of psychology.'

"Fifty years ago, the people of England were prosperous and secure. In those days, it seemed as if there was no limit to human progress. Every day in every way things got better and better. Taxation was low, labor was plentiful, and food was cheap. There was no Socialist nonsense then. The lower classes knew their place and were the happier for it. The whole trouble started when Labour members began to swamp the House of Commons. Our tradition is government by gentlemen, not by miners and shopkeepers, and from the moment the rabble was given power Britain began to decline. It is no good trying to run the country by pretending that everyone is equal. Look how the army has been ruined by all this talk about equality. The best officers are not those who can pass exams—any clever bank clerk's son can do that—but those who are born to command. It is the same with men as it is with animals: breeding always tells in the long run.

"The development of science, far from improving the lot of mankind, has helped to make the world a great deal less pleasant than it once was. It is true that medical knowledge has advanced and that people now live a lot longer than they once did, but discoveries like penicillin are only the exception which proves the rule. Anyway, what is the good of prolonging people's wretched existences if they have nothing worth living for? It is rather like operating on a condemned murderer to ensure that he is well enough to be hanged. What counts is not so much the quantity of life as its quality. 'Better fifty years of Europe than a cycle of Cathay.' If I were given the choice of forty years of life in the late nineteenth century or eighty years of life in the present age, I would not hesitate for one second. Any person possessing an atom of patriotism would be proud to have lived at a time when his country was esteemed throughout the world and when the proudest claim a man could make was that he was of British birth.

"If this country is ever to recover the reputation it once had, we must revive our spirit of independence, initiative, and honor. We must return to the days when an Englishman's word was his bond: when a check drawn on a London bank was regarded by foreigners as of greater worth than the negotiable currency of neighboring states. We must treat inferior races in the Empire with scrupulous fairness. We must spread abroad the blessings of liberty and self-government which have made this island justly famous and have earned our legislature the right to describe itself as the mother of parliaments. But we must on no account be stampeded into surrendering territories which our ancestors bought with their lives, and which through our endeavors have been so extensively enriched and enlarged."

Major Bigot's peroration was received with enthusiasm and he sat down amid loud applause. The chairman then called upon Mr. Hopewell to oppose the motion.

Mr. Hopewell began by congratulating Major Bigot

on his forceful and eloquent speech. "I do not, however, imagine," he said, "that many people here this evening will accept Major Bigot's verdict that the last fifty years have witnessed no improvements of any kind. On the contrary, I suspect that most of you will agree with me when I say that the history of the twentieth century is the history of progress. It is easy to appreciate why Major Bigot persists in believing as he does. He belongs to a class that has seen better days and that consequently always looks back with regret and forward with despair. It would be asking too much to expect him not to regard a decline in his personal standard of living as a symptom of a general relapse. The impoverished gentry may believe that they share the common lot, and that the country is rapidly going to the dogs, but workingmen have a very different story to tell. They know how greatly their condition has improved since the end of the Victorian era. When I say that no previous age can boast so many reforms and improvements as have been instituted during our lifetime, I rest my assertion not on the prejudices of a retired army officer, but upon the judgment and authority of the British people. The great changes we have witnessed in housing, sanitation, poor relief, public health, and education have all been effected by acts of Parliament, a fact which provides striking testimony to the beneficial nature of legislation. As no century rivals our own in the extent of its parliamentary activity, it stands to reason that no other age has improved so rapidly and radically as has ours.

"The point at issue is really very simple. When we consider the entertainments that we now enjoy: television, radio, the cinema, and motor cars; and when we remember the labor-saving devices, which deprive the day of so much of its former drudgery, machines like refrigerators, washing machines, and vacuum cleaners, it becomes obvious that we live easier and pleasanter lives than our grandparents did. Major Bigot said that science had done the world more harm than good. I would like to ask him one question. What possible harm have washing machines done?" Mr. Telling, who had vainly endeavored to catch the chairman's eye, at this point asked whether the opposer was aware that the motor car was invented before 1900. Despite cries of "Answer!" Mr. Hopewell ignored the interruption.

"Major Bigot has made much of the decline of the younger generation's manners and morals. It is, of course, perfectly true that some of the formality to which he may have become accustomed has disappeared during the last twenty years or so—and a very good thing, too. It is even possible that the old spirit of servility, which is what many people really refer to when they deplore the decay of civility, is on its way out. Happily, it seems probable that hypocrisy is no longer as fashionable as it once was. What is lost on the swings is more than gained on the roundabouts. There are few more significant signs of progress than the fact that children today are genuine and natural.

"The shocking barbarity of Major Bigot's proposals

for disciplining the young are too horrible to contemplate. It is only to be hoped that he did not intend them seriously. If one accepts the view that children require no greater degree of discipline than they get at present, and if one admits that their behavior on the whole leaves little to be desired, it follows that it is unnecessary and unjust to subject them to tyrannical authority. Modern psychology has reinforced the teaching of liberalism, for it shows that freedom is essential to the healthy growth of individuals. Parents should therefore be forbidden to warp their children's development by imposing superfluous restraints upon them. Better still, propagandists, like the proposer of this motion, should be prevented by law from disseminating their illiberal opinions.

"All the evidence goes to show that the modern world is a far better place in which to live than was the Victorian age. It is a healthier world. It provides a greater variety of entertainment. People are happier and far more secure. Science has annihilated distance. Wages have risen. Education has been extended and mankind is rapidly progressing toward a better and more civilized state." On the conclusion of Mr. Hopewell's speech, the debate was thrown open to the house, and the motion was finally carried by a small majority.

APPENDIX B

The Good Old Days (Re-examined)

The Great Muddle Debating Society of England met recently to discuss the motion: "This house regrets the passing of the good old days." The chairman called upon Major Bigot to propose. The Major began by describing England's position a few years before the turn of the century. "In those days," he said, "we possessed the greatest empire ever known. Our navy was twice as large as that of any other nation and we were by far the richest country in the world. Today, the position is not so happy. Our overseas possessions have been squandered by a rabble of fanatical bolshies . . ." At this point Mr. Promise asked the chairman whether it was in order to refer to a group of enlightened statesmen, who had freed the subject races of Asia from the ignominious yoke of imperialist rule in the disparaging terms employed by the proposer.[1] After some hesi-

[1] Major Bigot is obviously fond of using emotional language. He describes the Empire as "squandered by a rabble of fanatical bolshies." Presumably, such words were chosen to create a strong sense of disapproval of socialism. Mr. Promise, a supporter of left-wing policies, refers to exactly the same objec-

tation the chairman decided that the words complained of were permissible. "Our navy," continued the Major, "is nothing more than an appendage to the American fleet, and our budgets are only balanced by going to the United States, cap in hand, and begging for dollar loans.[2]

"Nobody in his right mind can deny that England was a very much better country to live in fifty years ago than it is today.[3] That the last half century has witnessed a sad decline in manners and enterprise is unfortunately self-evident.[4] Speaking as an army offi-

---

tive fact (i.e., that in 1947, parts of the Empire were granted self-rule by the Labour Government) in terms calculated to win acceptance of the policy. The Labour leaders, in his estimate, were a "group of enlightened statesmen." Whether Labour politicians are "fanatical bolshies" or "enlightened statesmen" is a question of facts, not words. See page 48.

[2] Major Bigot seeks to discredit the policy of dependence upon American aid by using words which suggest that it is humiliating and subservient, thus prejudicing the issue. See page 50.

[3] Whether this assertion is true or not is the point under discussion, and it cannot logically be decided by assuming what is to be proved. Prefacing dubious generalizations with the remark "Nobody in his right mind can deny that . . ." is a form of question begging. See page 53. The assertion moreover involves a veiled threat, since by implication anybody who persists in denying the proposition thereby admits he is not in his right mind, a distasteful admission to have to make. It also involves the *argumentum ad ignorantiam:* that is, the attempt to prove propositions by maintaining that they have never been disproved. See page 104.

[4] Settled questions and unchallenged prejudices are frequently defended on the ground that they are self-evident. What is plain to one person, however, is not necessarily clear

cer with some small experience of men, I do not hesitate to say that modern soldiers are mentally, physically, and morally inferior to the troops I commanded as a young subaltern during the first World War.[5] The difference is one of upbringing. Parents today allow their children to do whatever they like. Boys of fourteen are allowed to smoke and drink. The rod is spared and the child is spoiled.[6] Juvenile delinquency would cease to be a serious problem if magistrates were authorized to sentence young offenders to birching.[7] I well remember a boy whom I employed shortly after the first World War telling me that a flogging he received for stealing apples had given him a lesson

---

to another. Anyway, if the evidence is so striking, there can be no harm in asking to be shown it. Too many fallacies owe their survival to this defense for it to remain unchallenged. See page 30.

[5] Major Bigot's appeal to his professional prestige lends some authority to his dogmatizing but is a poor substitute for an argument. We should not be deceived by the phrase "with some small experience of men." The assumed modesty is part of the conspiracy. See page 60.

[6] An argument is not clinched by the use of a slogan. Major Bigot may be right in thinking that children at present are given too much freedom, but the belief that discipline can best be achieved by the rod is not established merely by reference to a proverb. See page 71.

[7] Major Bigot is now astride one of his favorite hobbyhorses and it is not therefore surprising that he has wandered some way from the point. See page 102. His views on juvenile delinquency involve an absurd oversimplification both of the problem and its remedy. See page 71. Major Bigot clearly reveals his tendency to see everything in black and white, and his fondness for reaching conclusions when the evidence only justifies suspended judgment.

he would never forget. It just goes to show that a good hiding is the only thing boys understand.[8]

"Unfortunately, nowadays, we have discarded the precepts of Solomon and seem to prefer the wisdom of Professor Freud. It is my considered opinion that no man is more to blame for our present difficulties than the so-called 'father of psychology.' [9]

"Fifty years ago, the people of England were prosperous and secure. In those days, it seemed as if there was no limit to human progress. Every day in every way things got better and better. Taxation was low, labor was plentiful and food was cheap. There was no Socialist nonsense then. The lower classes knew their place and were the happier for it.[10] The whole trouble started when Labour members began to swamp the House of Commons. Our tradition is government by gentlemen, not by miners and shopkeepers, and from the moment the rabble was given

[8] It shows nothing of the sort. Even if we accept the thesis that boys understand a good thrashing, that does not mean that it is the only thing they understand. Major Bigot is generalizing from insufficient evidence. His garden boy's comment may not represent the views of other boys. See page 82.

[9] Finding scapegoats is a characteristic device of thinkers who incline to oversimplify problems. See page 70.

[10] Major Bigot's idyllic description of England at the turn of the century depends upon partial selection of the evidence. When he claims that "people" fifty years ago were secure and prosperous, he overlooks the large number of unemployed, he forgets that old-age pensions had not been introduced and that medical attention was financially beyond most working men's reach. Major Bigot was probably only thinking of the gentry when he referred to the security and prosperity of the "people."

power Britain began to decline.[11] It is no good trying to run the country by pretending that everyone is equal. Look how the army has been ruined by all this talk about equality. The best officers are not those who can pass exams—any clever bank clerk's son can do that—but those who are born to command.[12] It is the same with men as it is with animals: breeding always tells in the long run.[13]

"The development of science, far from improving the lot of mankind, has helped to make the world a great deal less pleasant than it once was. It is true that medical knowledge has advanced and that people now live a lot longer than they once did, but discoveries like penicillin are only the exception which

[11] This remark obviously manifests blinding prejudice. It combines the fallacy of believing that there is only *one* cause of a problem, see page 72; the fallacy of oversimplification, see page 71; the fallacy of blaming scapegoats for every disaster, see page 70; and the fallacy of *post hoc, propter hoc,* see page 87.

[12] Major Bigot obviously belongs to the category of officers born to command. He opposes examinations because they constitute a threat to a hereditary class famous more for its breeding than its intelligence. Prejudice often arises from threatened vested interests. See page 31.

[13] The analogy depends upon an unsound comparison and is manifestly a rationalization. It is perfectly true that selective breeding improves animals physically. The development of the human mind, however, depends on environment. A horse will be equally swift if bred in France or England, other things being equal. But a man's character will be greatly affected by the opinions prevailing in the country in which he grows up, his parent's outlook, and other factors of the kind. It is not good breeding that makes good officers, but good training.

proves the rule.[14] Anyway, what is the good of prolonging people's wretched existences if they have nothing worth living for? It is rather like operating on a condemned murderer to ensure that he is well enough to be hanged. What counts is not so much the quantity of life as its quality. 'Better fifty years of Europe than a cycle of Cathay.' If I were given the choice of forty years of life in the late nineteenth century or eighty years of life in the present age, I would not hesitate for one second. Any person possessing an atom of patriotism would be proud to have lived at a time when his country was esteemed throughout the world and when the proudest claim a man could make was that he was of British birth.[15]

"If this country is ever to recover the reputation it once had, we must revive our spirit of independence, initiative, and honor. We must return to the days when an Englishman's word was his bond: when a check drawn on a London bank was regarded by foreigners as of greater worth than the negotiable currency of neighboring states. We must treat inferior races in the Empire with scrupulous fairness. We must spread abroad the blessings of liberty and self-government which have made this island justly famous and have earned our legislature the right to

[14] It is difficult to understand how the discovery of health-giving drugs proves the rule that science has made the world more disagreeable. The phrase is, of course, meaningless. See page 85.

[15] This is an example of the *argumentum ad populum*. See page 57.

describe itself as the mother of parliaments. But we must on no account be stampeded into surrendering territories which our ancestors bought with their lives, and which through our endeavors have been so extensively enriched and enlarged." [16]

Major Bigot's peroration was received with enthusiasm and he sat down amid loud applause. The chairman then called upon Mr. Hopewell to oppose the motion.

Mr. Hopewell began by congratulating Major Bigot on his forceful and eloquent speech. "I do not, however, imagine," he said, "that many people here this evening will accept Major Bigot's verdict that the last fifty years have witnessed no improvements of any kind.[17] On the contrary, I suspect that most of you will agree with me when I say that the history of the twentieth century is the history of progress. It is easy to appreciate why Major Bigot persists in believing as he does. He belongs to a class that has seen better days and that consequently always looks back with regret and forward with despair. It would be asking too much to expect him not to regard a

[16] Major Bigot has preserved his mental harmony by keeping two incompatible ideas in watertight compartments. He talks about propagating "ideas of liberty and self-government," and then later says that Britain must on no account surrender any part of her Empire, or in other words grant self-government. See page 15.

[17] Major Bigot said many silly things during the course of his speech, but he did not in fact go as far as Mr. Hopewell alleges. Mr. Hopewell, by unwarrantably extending his opponent's argument, diminishes the force of his own case. See page 73.

decline in his personal standard of living as a symptom of a general relapse.[18] The impoverished gentry may believe that they share the common lot, and that the country is rapidly going to the dogs, but workingmen have a very different story to tell. They know how greatly their condition has improved since the end of the Victorian era. When I say that no previous age can boast so many reforms and improvements as have been instituted during our lifetime, I rest my assertion not on the prejudices of a retired army officer, but upon the judgment and authority of the British people.[19] The great changes we have witnessed in housing, sanitation, poor relief, public health, and education have all been effected by acts of Parliament, a fact which provides striking testimony to the beneficial nature of legislation. As no century rivals our own in the extent of its parliamentary activity, it stands to reason that no other age has improved so rapidly and radically as has ours.[20]

[18] This is an example of the *argumentum ad hominem*. Mr. Hopewell is probably right in assuming that Major Bigot's views are colored by his personal circumstances and upbringing. But as prejudiced people can be right, and impartial people are sometimes wrong, Major Bigot's arguments are not demolished by the discovery that he is biassed. See page 102.

[19] Mr. Hopewell's appeal to the authority of the British people is an example of the *argumentum ad verecundiam*. See page 61.

[20] This argument asserts that *all* improvements are effected by legislation. But as medical discoveries, to take only one example, are made by scientists, not politicians, there are changes for the better which cannot be attributed to acts of Parliament. The most that can reasonably be asserted is that

"The point at issue is really very simple. When we consider the entertainments that we now enjoy: television, radio, the cinema, and motor cars; and when we remember the labor-saving devices, which deprive the day of so much of its former drudgery, machines like refrigerators, washing machines, and vacuum cleaners, it becomes obvious that we live easier and pleasanter lives than our grandparents did. Major Bigot said that science had done the world more harm than good. I would like to ask him one question. What possible harm have washing machines done?" [21] Mr. Telling, who had vainly endeavored to catch the chairman's eye, at this point asked whether the opposer was aware that the motor car was invented before 1900.[22] Despite cries of "Answer!" Mr. Hopewell ignored the interruption.

---

some improvements originate from the House of Commons. See page 85. Mr. Hopewell also commits himself to the fallacy of the undistributed middle. His argument translated into symbols reads: "Some A is produced by B, therefore B produces A." If the second part of the proposition read: "therefore some B produces A," it would be true but tautologous. See page 82.

[21] This rhetorical question completely evades the point. Major Bigot never denied that science was sometimes beneficial. What he argued was that on balance it did more harm than good. See page 72.

[22] Presumably, the point of this interruption was to discredit Mr. Hopewell's argument by indicating the falsehood of an incidental statement it happened to contain. That the motor car, or cinema for that matter, was invented before 1900, in no way affects the argument that there are more amusements now than there were then. See page 103.

"Major Bigot has made much of the decline of the younger generation's manners and morals. It is, of course, perfectly true that some of the formality to which he may have become accustomed has disappeared during the last twenty years or so—and a very good thing, too. It is even possible that the old spirit of servility, which is what many people really refer to when they deplore the decay of civility, is on its way out. Happily, it seems probable that hypocrisy is no longer as fashionable as it once was. What is lost on the swings is more than gained on the roundabouts. There are few more significant signs of progress than the fact that children today are genuine and natural.[23]

"The shocking barbarity of Major Bigot's proposals for disciplining the young are too horrible to contemplate. It is only to be hoped that he did not intend them seriously.[24] If one accepts the view that children require no greater degree of discipline than they get at present, and if one admits that their behavior on the whole leaves little to be desired, it follows that it is unnecessary and unjust to subject them to tyran-

[23] Mr. Hopewell fails to define the words he uses. Whether being "natural" is evidence of regress or progress depends upon what is meant by "natural." The "natural" instincts of man provoke him to theft, murder, and rape, and to give such instincts free rein would not generally be regarded as progressive. See page 44. In this context the word "significant" is an unfinished term. See page 48.

[24] This is an example of evading the point by resorting to being shocked.

nical authority.[25] Modern psychology has reinforced the teaching of liberalism, for it shows that freedom is essential to the healthy growth of individuals. Parents should therefore be forbidden to warp their children's development by imposing superfluous restraints upon them. Better still, propagandists, like the proposer of this motion, should be prevented by law from disseminating their illiberal opinions.[26]

"All the evidence goes to show that the modern world is a far better place in which to live than was the Victorian age. It is a healthier world. It provides a greater variety of entertainment. People are happier and far more secure. Science has annihilated distance. Wages have risen. Education has been extended and mankind is rapidly progressing toward a better and more civilized state." [27] On the conclusion of Mr. Hopewell's speech, the debate was thrown open to the house, and the motion was finally carried by a small majority.

[25] This is a circular argument. In effect what has been said is: if discipline is unnecessary it is unnecessary. See page 52.

[26] Mr. Hopewell here resorts to special pleading. He first maintains that freedom is essential to the full development of individuals, and then proposes to silence his opponents by act of Parliament. See page 40.

[27] The evidence is obviously being forced to conform to a preconceived pattern. Much has been omitted. Wages may have risen, but so have costs, and science having annihilated distance, has thus made atomic rockets feasible.

Books for Further Reading

CHASE, STUART. *The Tyranny of Words.* Harcourt, Brace and Co., 1938.

CRAWSHAY-WILLIAMS, RUPERT. *The Comforts of Unreason.* Routledge and Kegan Paul Ltd., 1947.

FIELD, GUY CROMWELL. *Prejudice and Impartiality.* Robert M. McBride and Co., 1932.

GLOVER, WILLIAM. *Know Your Own Mind.* Macmillan Co., 1914.

HART, BERNARD. *The Psychology of Insanity.* Cambridge University Press, 1941.

HOWARD, B. A. *The Proper Study of Mankind.* Ginn and Co., 1933.

JEPSON, R. W. *Clear Thinking.* Longmans, Green and Co., 1955.

——— *Teach Yourself to Think.* English Universities Press, 1949.

MANDER, ALFRED E. *Clearer Thinking.* C. A. Watts and Co., 1949.

ROBINSON, JAMES HARVEY. *The Mind in the Making.* Harper & Brothers, 1921.

STEBBING, L. S. *Thinking to Some Purpose.* Penguin Books, 1959.

THOULESS, ROBERT H. *Straight and Crooked Thinking.* English Universities Press, 1950.

TROTTER, WILFRED. *Instincts of the Herd in Peace and War.* Oxford University Press, 1953.

Index